Praise for
Unlocking Your Family Patterns

Written by long-standing friends of the AACC, these seminary-trained clinicians bring their best insights to Unlocking Your Family Patterns. *These guys know what they are talking about, and this book will guide you on life's journey so that you don't repeat what you didn't like about some of your own family experiences. Starting with famous families of the Bible, you will begin to understand why each of us, in our own families, needs daily help to do things differently.* Unlocking Your Family Patterns *will walk you through that journey.*

> —Dr. Tim Clinton, president,
> American Association of Christian Counselors

DR. HENRY CLOUD | DR. JOHN TOWNSEND
DAVE CARDER | DR. EARL HENSLIN

Unlocking
Your Family Patterns

Finding Freedom from a Hurtful Past

MOODY PUBLISHERS
CHICAGO

All Scripture quotations, unless otherwise indicated, are taken from the *New American Standard Bible*®, Copyright © 1960, 1962, 1963, 1968, 1971, 1972, 1973, 1975, 1977, 1995 by The Lockman Foundation. Used by permission. (www.Lockman.org)

Scripture quotations marked NIV are taken from the Holy Bible, New International Version®, NIV®. Copyright © 1973, 1978, 1984 by Biblica, Inc.™ Used by permission of Zondervan. All rights reserved worldwide.

Scripture quotations marked NLT are taken from the *Holy Bible, New Living Translation,* copyright © 1996. Used by permission of Tyndale House Publishers, Inc., Wheaton, Illinois 60189, U.S.A. All rights reserved.

Scripture quotations marked KJV are taken from the King James Version.

Scripture quotations marked *The Message* are from *The Message,* copyright © by Eugene H. Peterson 1993, 1994, 1995. Used by permission of NavPress Publishing Group.

Edited by: Annette LaPlaca
Cover design: Thinkpen Design
Interior design: Smartt Guys design

Library of Congress Cataloging-in-Publication Data
Unlocking your family patterns : finding freedom from a hurtful past / Henry
Cloud ... [et al.]. -- [New ed.]
     p. cm.
Rev. ed. of: Secrets of your family tree. 1991
Includes bibliographical references.
ISBN 978-0-8024-7744-6
1. Families--Religious life. 2. Dysfunctional families. I. Cloud, Henry.
II. Cloud, Henry. Secrets of your family tree. III. Title: Finding freedom
from a hurtful past.
BV4526.3.U55 2011
248.8'6--dc22
                          2010050098

We hope you enjoy this book from Moody Publishers. Our goal is to provide high-quality, thought-provoking books and products that connect truth to your real needs and challenges. For more information on other books and products written and produced from a biblical perspective, go to www.moodypublishers.com or write to:

Moody Publishers
820 N. LaSalle Boulevard
Chicago, IL 60610

3 5 7 9 10 8 6 4

Printed in the United States of America

Contents

Part 3
FAMILY HEALTH: HOW TO DO IT RIGHT WHEN YOU LEARNED IT WRONG

Foreword

HOW times have changed!

Back in the forties when I was a boy, the church and Christian circles had neither time nor tolerance for life's raw realities. Words such as rape and incest, homosexuality, and child molestation were never heard from the pulpit and seldom, if ever, discussed in small groups. Those who were the involuntary victims of divorce or the objects of brutality were left to suffer in silence, feeling alienated and ashamed.

By the time I entered the ministry in the early sixties, the evangelical Christian community was a bit more open and realistic but still guarded and certainly reluctant to get involved. Families who struggled could find perhaps a caring pastor or a compassionate counselor, but the hope of receiving help from support groups in the church was virtually nonexistent. Those in the church who wrestled with an addiction were more often than not told to confess their sins and get a grip on themselves. And it wasn't uncommon for preachers to use the Bible as the basis for such exhortations. If the troubled individuals didn't "snap out of it," they were labeled as "sick" or, worse, "rebellious."

The painful truth has finally been allowed to come out of the closet. At long last, pastors and congregations have stopped whispering and started addressing the secret struggles that plague many, if not most, families. Rather than pounding pulpits and demanding instant change, we have acknowledged that dysfunctional families are often in the church, that recovery takes time and is a painful process, and, in fact, that the process cannot be accelerated by cramming more and more convicting Scriptures down the throat of the abandoned or the abused. Guilt and shame are not friends of grace that prompt inner healing.

One of the benefits emerging from the long-awaited and much-needed change is a growing number of books that are designed to help those who hurt find healing. Unfortunately, many of these books are long on psychology and short on theology. The timeless principles of God's Word are eclipsed by human reasoning and man-made techniques and conclusions. They may sound plausible and make good sense, but they lack the power to effect lasting recovery. Frequently, these books reflect the bias of one author's pet hobbyhorse.

The book you hold in your hand is different. It is the result of four authors' work, not one. It has been written by those regularly in touch with reality, not dreamers dabbling in theory. Furthermore, it is based on the rock-hard truths of Scripture, not the sandy soil of nice-sounding ideas and suggestions dredged up from a collection of academic textbooks. Again and again you will find biblical examples and scriptural references, but they fit; they aren't forced. This balanced approach reassures the reader that he or she is not being led astray.

But don't think this is just another book on troubled families. This one is hard-hitting, insightful, unpredictable, direct, and refreshingly candid. Best of all, it is realistic. The book promises no super-quick fixes, no sure-fire guarantees, and no airtight solutions. It does, however, confront the issues that must be addressed, and it does ask the questions that need to be answered in order to find recovery.

I am encouraged that you are about to discover some essential secrets of your family story and that the all-important process of inner healing will soon be under way. Consider yourself fortunate to be living in the twenty-first century. It is doubtful that a book this straightforward would have even been published fifty years ago. If it had been, most in the church would never have read it.

I'm glad times have changed!

Chuck Swindoll
Pastor, Author, Radio Bible Teacher

Introduction

Dave Carder

EVEN AT twenty-nine, Julie vividly remembered the countless Thursdays at school when she realized with horror that she had forgotten to do her early morning chore at home. Thursday was "vacuuming day" for her mother, and Julie's job before she left for school was to put on top of her bed everything usually stored underneath it. With overwhelming sickness and fear she knew what lay in store for her when she came home.

How could I have forgotten again? she agonized. And if her mind was so forgetful, why couldn't she ever forget the look on Dad's face when he found out? Why did Mom always have to tell Dad when he got home that she had forgotten?

And why did it seem that everything went in slow motion when Dad began to punish her? Even as he was pulling his belt out of his pants' belt loops, it seemed to take forever. It was like a horror movie in painful freeze-frame.

And why, dear God, why did she, a fourteen-year-old girl, have to disrobe totally?

Even now she could see the pattern on the old linoleum floor, only inches from her face as she lay over that cold kitchen chair. She remembered begging for mercy and promising to reform in the same breath, but it was always hopeless.

Julie's lying across the chair was the signal for her two older brothers to enter the kitchen and watch the macabre family ritual. Her father said that having them see what happened to her would help them not to make the same mistake themselves.

Then the blows would start. The abuse was almost incomprehensible in its horror and duration. It often ended with her either vomiting or urinating on the floor. Then everybody walked out. When she had finished her soul-rending sobs, she was expected to clean herself up, along with her mess. Then it was back to business as usual, with Dad often returning to his office at the church that evening.

Left alone with her pain into adulthood, Julie became consumed with finding ways to sedate it. She had to numb it at all cost. A sense of rage lurked constantly just beneath the surface of her emotions and occasionally flared up if she didn't keep it stifled. On other occasions the pain would leave her so depressed she could hardly function.

It wasn't long until she got the nickname "Wild One." She drank to excess and slept around. As a nursing student, she found access to pharmaceuticals that helped temporarily. She figured out ways to get the drugs on the sly, even if that meant keeping them from patients who desperately needed their pain-killing properties. She started racing four-wheel-drive vehicles on weekends, and the rowdy relationships that spun out of hanging with that crowd eventually destroyed her marriage.

Desperate for a new relationship to ease the pain, she remarried with hardly a thought about the consequences. She bore a child, which resulted in extra responsibilities. The religious training she had received in her youth began to appeal to her as a source of relief from her pain, but her new husband had no interest in such matters. In yet another attempt to reach out for help in her prolonged agony, she decided to attend church by herself. Fortunately, she chose a church that was open to and understanding of the process of recovery.

Julie is an adult coping with the effects of a dysfunctional family background. Although it is obvious that a parent should not beat a child over failure to clear things out from under a bed, Julie's situation is, tragically, not uncommon, even among Christian families. Her dad's overreaction, her mother's inability to confront her daughter directly about a household chore, the terrible shaming effect of being nude as a young teen in front of her brothers, the fact that nobody ever talked about the beatings, that everybody learned to shut down his feelings, and that everyone left the family to enter into troubled and broken marriages all describe the characteristic patterns of a dysfunctional family.

Those patterns are often easier to see in other families than to recognize in your own; that is exactly what the first three chapters of this book are about. Most of you will be familiar with the biblical families we discuss, so it makes sense to look at them first. Besides, most Christians tend to over-sanctify the families described in the Bible, so there is new ground to cover in terms of seeing them in a different, more realistic light. God's Word has some helpful things to say regarding their behavior and its consequences in their family trees.

As you work through this book, you may find yourself resisting and even denying the dysfunctionality described. That is not surprising, since this is painful material, and all of our families are dysfunctional to one degree or another. But don't be tempted to let that discomfort serve as an excuse to stop the journey of discovery. Healthy, God-honoring behavior and relationships are too important.

You may feel that your family of origin wasn't dysfunctional since your father wasn't an alcoholic, or even a "rage-aholic," as Julie's father was. The truth is, however, that, due to the fallen nature of all parents (and children), all families are flawed and therefore dysfunctional to a certain degree. Addictive and compulsive behaviors (addictions to food, sex, work, and so on) are extremely common in even "the best families," and such behavior is almost always linked to some form of troubled family background. We believe the vast majority of readers will benefit from studying the concepts presented in this book, whether for help in their own lives or for the sake of ministering to friends, business associates, or loved ones.

Remember, too, that it is common for multiple siblings raised in the same family system to perceive that family very differently. Your brother or sister might have such a different view of your family that you wonder if he or she is remembering the same group of people you do! Chapters 4 and 5 will look at what happens within families that causes children to see their family of origin so differently.

Everyone outside Julie's family saw it as a normal family, but Julie's family had a secret. That secret was made more powerful by the realization that if word of the beatings got out, her dad could lose his place of leadership in the church. Worse yet, the ultimate humiliation for a Christian family, he might go to jail. The unique stresses and tensions within the families of vocational Christian workers (pastors, missionaries, parachurch workers, and so on) are the focus of the first appendix. Almost every moral failure in the ministry has a family history to it that few are aware of. Even observers within the family that produced the Christian worker would not link family patterns with individual sins, but this book will show otherwise.

Julie's mother took the role of the "enabler." She did exactly what the term says: She enabled the family system to function the way it did. If she had not reported Julie's failures to her father, little would have happened. In addition, by not holding her husband accountable for his cruel behavior, she gave tacit approval to the physical and sexual abuse. If she did protest and he refused to listen, she should have sought outside help for the family. Yet, for systemic reasons, she could not or would not. In any case, she did not.

Strange as it may sound, the cycle of forgetting, with its punishment, served Julie in a needs-based way. She suffered from an extreme lack of attention and love from her parents, and the harsh punishment served as a form of attention, however excessive and abusive, from her parents. An unwritten rule in a dysfunctional family is that it is better to be picked on than to be ignored. By way of the abuse, at least everybody knew Julie existed.

The pattern of abuse actually became predictable in Julie's family. As bizarre as it might sound, everybody in the family *needed* to have Julie forget to put her stuff on top of the bed. Dad needed to release his rage, Mom needed to be in control of the family, Julie needed to know that she was important in this otherwise emotionally sterile family, and her brothers needed someone to bear the family anger and shame, someone to be the "family scapegoat," so that they could feel safe and unafraid that Dad might blow up at them. This pattern is typical of dysfunctional family systems, and it is all too familiar to adults who come from such a background.

Julie's mother's own pain grew so intense that she took a job as far away from home as she could commute in one day. That job served as a haven for her; it became her "other world." For her, going to work spelled *freedom.* Julie's mom's separation from the pain-filled family contributed to the emotional alienation at home. As is often the case, the family's general emotional void led to inappropriate sexual relationships between Julie and her brothers. Sadly and shockingly, it even led to one incestuous experience with her mom.

As we examine Julie's family of origin, the list of "family secrets" grows, and an interesting phenomenon emerges. Julie, who felt like the least important member of the family, who served as the "identified patient" (a term explored more fully in chapter 4), who felt so victimized and helpless, was actually the most powerful figure in the family system. She knew enough about everyone in the family to destroy each of them, should the information leak. But because she felt so helpless and so responsible, she couldn't perceive herself as having any power. The pain and hurt had "gone underground" in Julie and had become what counselors call "unfinished business." It was impossible for her actually to leave home emotionally. Oh, she could leave physically, and she did so as soon as it was legal, but when she left she took all the family's secrets with her along with their unfinished business, which contributed to her agony in adulthood.

It was exhausting for Julie to carry her family's secrets and unfinished business inside her heart. A pattern of depression, alcoholism, wild partying, and even abortions developed. Instead of finding relief, she only compounded the pain. This rage of no relief had to be tranquilized. Any solution, no matter how temporary or unhealthy, seemed acceptable.

Only in desperation, when God appeared to be the last of what had been a number of hopes, did she come back to faith. Yet that salvation experience in adulthood did not by itself do away with the unfinished business in Julie's life, as so many modern-day critics of Christian counseling mistakenly believe it should have.

It did not, and it could not. It is Christianized wishful thinking for people who have never experienced serious emotional damage, or recovery, to assert that therapy for persons who have been injured isn't necessary, that all they need is Jesus. Now it is true that sometimes God does deliver an individual in one moment from vast amounts of pain accumulated in the past, but that is not the norm. Instead, consequences from the past carry over into the present, even after the person receives Christ. The Lord wants us to work on changing the hurtful thinking and behaviors of the past and put on godliness in the present. We will look at this matter more fully later, principally in chapter 4. Suffice it to say for now that Julie's step back toward God was a critical first step.

Julie's salvation experience initially increased the load she bore. She had a great deal of unfinished business to do with God first. After all, her biological father was one of God's representatives on earth. How and why he went into the ministry, the kind of church he chose, the kind of people who chose the church he pastored—all those are the focus of chapter 6. Since churches are made up of families, it only makes sense that they often operate exactly like the family-of-origin pattern of the dominant leader and/or the congregants. Many of us select the church system we do because of the unfinished business we carry from our families of origin.

The modern family faces challenges and threats unlike those any previous generation experienced. Shocking divorce statistics, rising numbers of incest victims, surging increases in incidents of abuse, and the presence of multitudes of single adults afraid to marry (or remarry) after observing the pain around them—all are symptomatic of a society responding to, and inundated with, trauma.

Is this book just another depressing review of the downward trend of the family? Absolutely not! As Christian ministers and counselors we are wholeheartedly committed to recovery, to healing, and to restoration of relationships—all of which can lead to healthy new patterns for the future. We dare to think it is possible for the next generation to have a better family environment than the current generation. That is why a major thrust of this book is looking at healthy—godly—family living.

Is this just another book on codependence? Well, yes and no. Yes, because codependence and other similar patterns play a part in family dysfunction. And no, because the book doesn't offer a general look at codependence. The book focuses instead on the roots of dysfunctional and codependent behavior and relationships by examining family systems first in the light of Scripture and then in the light of family systems and recovery theory and experience.

This book is not based on untested theory. As a result of the breadth of experience and ministry of the authors, you will find chapters 7 through 11 (and the very helpful appendices) practical, biblical, and capable of delivering exactly what the section title says about developing family health: how to do it right when you learned it wrong.

Throughout the book, you will find thought-provoking, challenging input from the Bible. At the end of each chapter we have provided review questions and exercises to help you whether you do them by yourself or in a group setting. We are praying that many groups will study this book and use the study questions to spark discussion. We urge you to personalize the study questions by writing down on the page (yes, we're giving you permission to write in this book) any insights the Lord may give you as you prayerfully consider the concepts discussed. We hope that while you process the concepts in this book you will feel an inner urge to explore your own family tree and develop insight into your present family system.

One final caution: This is not a book that explores only highly abusive families. Though Julie's story starts us on our journey, it is important to remember that *this is a book about ordinary families in ordinary, everyday struggles.* Family patterns don't have to be extraordinary to be powerful. Family patterns can be simple, but they are always significant. Such "secrets" are the things, events, or people that are "off limits" to family discussion or discussion with outsiders. They are the things strictly subject to the official "party line" of the family—that family system's interpretation of behavior and relationships.

Family secrets are often common, everyday occurrences that are painful and shameful (and unchangeable) for the child who experiences them:

a mother who goes to work and a young child who feels abandoned; parents who get divorced and the child who feels torn; a father who is physically or emotionally absent and the child who, as a result, feels ignored.

Often these circumstances (and many others like them) are inescapable, so please keep in mind that we are not trying to make anyone feel guilty. We want to encourage those of you who hurt, who wonder if there is any relief available for the pain, who desire to do family things less painfully, to step out and start the journey of understanding your past so that you can choose to live the present differently. We hope you will find our combined efforts in this book helpful and health-giving and, as a consequence, glorifying to our heavenly Father, who wants to heal our hurts.

Jesus said, "You will know the truth, and the truth will make you free" (John 8:32), and it is for this reason we have put this book together. He is the Truth, and He wants us to deal in truth with ourselves and our loved ones. We want the truth about you and your family to flood into and overrun the secrets that keep you in bondage to dysfunctional behavior and relationships.

May God bless you as you read these pages. One thing we are all sure of: The pain of discovery, and recovery, will be worth it.

PART ONE

DYSFUNCTION IN FAMILIES OF THE BIBLE

1

David and His Family Tree

Earl Henslin

WHILE LIVING AT home after his college graduation, Ron found himself obsessed with his half-sister, Marita, who was home from college for the summer. Every time Ron watched her walk through the house, his desire grew. Marita was agonizingly beautiful.

Ron felt confused and ashamed. How could he lust after his own sister? Then he began to rationalize. After all, she wasn't his full sister. He'd been a proud big brother when Marita was a little girl, but now she was a gorgeous young woman, the object of his unceasing fantasies.

One morning Ron woke up depressed and guilt-ridden, knowing his obsessive desire was wrong. But desire overcame conscience, and soon he began to justify a plan to satisfy the unrelenting lust. After all, their dad had never been faithful to his mom or Marita's mother. He'd even once had an affair with the wife of a treasured employee. Dad approached beautiful women the same way he tackled his successful business: He saw what he wanted and went after it.

So, the first time Ron found himself alone in the house with Marita, he feigned a fever and called out for her to bring him something cool to drink. Unsuspecting, Marita was genuinely concerned. She had once or twice felt uneasy recently about the way Ron had been looking at her, but she chalked it up to her imagination.

Watching from his bedroom door, Ron was mesmerized by Marita's graceful movements around the family kitchen. As soon as Marita came near Ron's bed, he grabbed her.

Ron's body was pressed against Marita's before she could recover from the shock. He was kissing her and touching her in inappropriate ways. She cried out, but no one was home to hear. Marita tried to fight, but Ron was stronger and prevailed. Ron forcefully and brutally raped his sister.

Afterward Ron looked at Marita with a mixture of guilt and growing disgust. For some reason he couldn't bear to look at her anymore. A strange contempt overtook him once his lust had been satiated. He hurriedly slipped on a pair of jeans, then he practically threw Marita out of his room and locked the door.

Outside Marita cried and screamed while pulling her ripped clothing around her as tightly as she could in a desperate, futile effort also to cover her raw, wounded heart. She felt her very soul had been torn apart, violated, ashamed, used, and ruined. She'd saved her body for the husband she'd dreamed of having someday; now that gift had been soiled forever.

Her assault was avenged, however. When word got out about what had happened, Marita's brother Andrew decided to get even. He waited for two full years in the hope that their father would confront and deal with Ron, but when his dad did nothing, Andrew tracked Ron down and, in an act of pent-up fury, viciously murdered Ron for violating their sister.

This story did not come out of my counseling experiences, nor did it come from the pages of a supermarket tabloid. It is the shocking but true story of King David's family, right out of the Bible. Ron, Marita, and Andrew are actually David's eldest son Amnon, his daughter Tamar, and a younger son, Absalom (2 Samuel 13).

The foundation for Amnon's behavior was probably laid earlier in David's affair with Bathsheba. The David and Bathsheba story is familiar to most Christians. David sees Bathsheba bathing on the roof of her home, has her brought to the palace, and sleeps with her. She becomes pregnant, and—to cover up his guilt—David secretly orders that her husband, Uriah, be sent to the most dangerous part of the battlefield, where he is killed. Bathsheba then comes into David's household as his wife. The baby she is carrying is born and dies. We see David mourning and expressing deep grief over the loss of his son (2 Samuel 12:14–23), finally owning his part in the tragedies.

Amnon, Tamar, and Absalom were teenagers when the Bathsheba and David incident happened. They saw their father model behavior that was manipulative and treacherous: covering up his sin with Bathsheba by secretly giving the orders that led to Uriah's death. What those teenagers learned was how to cover up, how to not face issues, and how to ignore the hurt that grew out of one's actions. The stage was set for a thoroughly dysfunctional family history to unfold.

Part of the tragedy of David's family is that it never truly dealt with the incest between Amnon and Tamar. Time went by after the attack, two years in fact, and David still had taken no disciplinary action against Amnon. So Absalom took matters into his own hands. He invited his father and the family to his house for a party; the sheep shearing was over and a celebration was in order. Amnon went to his brother's house for the party—and, after Amnon had been drinking heavily, Absalom killed him. Absalom took pride in the murder, for he felt he'd finally avenged his sister's rape. But because he knew his crime would not go unpunished, he fled and was in exile from his family for three years (2 Samuel 13:23–38).

CONCEPTS THAT CAN LEAD TO HEALING

Stop and think about it. What did you learn about Absalom in Sunday school when you were growing up? Probably that Absalom was the "bad guy." He is usually seen as the scapegoat, supposedly the only one in David's family who had problems. It is easy to dump all the problems and responsibilities of a family on a single member. Yet when we look at David's family we can see that the whole family needed to deal with a number of issues. Let's look at a few of them:

1. *Each member of the family has hurts. Each member of the family needs help.*

There is no such thing as a scapegoat.

It is easy for a family to designate one of its members the family scapegoat. In the story just told, Absalom is the obvious "black sheep" of the family.

But in reality Absalom was not the only one in the family who needed help. He just "acted out" in the most obvious ways. There was something broken in David himself that prevented him from taking appropriate steps to deal with Amnon or fully to address the damage done to Tamar. And the emotional damage to Tamar was great. After the molestation, she lived the rest of her life in desolation (2 Samuel 13:20). She never married or had children, which was, in her culture, the ultimate disgrace. The pain of Amnon's violation devastated her whole life.

In all families each member has hurts and wounds; each member of the family needs help. Though we may consider some members of the family the scapegoats or label them the "bad guys," in reality all members of the family share the pain and, to varying degrees, the responsibility.

This principle was first applied in the treatment of alcohol and drug addiction. If only the alcoholic is treated and no one else in the family gets help, there is a higher rate of relapse than when the whole family is involved in treatment. It takes tough work to help family members see that "scapegoating" is counterproductive and that all share the pain.

Take Mark, for example. He was an eight-year-old boy who was failing in school and constantly fighting with the other boys on the playground. As it turned out, Mark had an older brother, Simon, who was "just perfect." He made straight As and was well liked by everyone. His "goodness" was so pronounced he held himself aloof from his little brother, whom he saw as "just a troublemaker." Their mother also spoke of Simon as if he wore a halo and wings. Their dad, an alcoholic, was basically absent from the family, only showing up randomly and often disappointing both of his sons with numerous "no shows" on days they'd anticipated seeing him. Both boys felt the same pain, but one dealt with it by trying to be perfect, the other by acting out.

With the help of a sympathetic family counselor, Mark and Simon both began to accept and grieve the difficult truth that their dad was never going to be there for them as long as the chronic illness of alcoholism had control of his life. The mom began to see her role in playing favorites and began to drop that dysfunctional game, instead treating the boys with equal love, respect, and concern. In time, healing happened. No more labels or "scapegoats"—just a family learning to deal with reality in healthier ways.

2. As parents we do the best we know how to do.

David was furious at what Amnon did to Tamar (2 Samuel 13:21), but the Scripture does not indicate that he did anything about it. For Tamar to regain her self-respect, she needed her father to take her violation and hurt seriously and take some clear protective action. David was a godly man yet he did not know how to face pain in his family directly and deal with it in a healthy, proactive way.

When David's son Absalom fled after killing Amnon (2 Samuel 13:38), David remained passive in addressing hurts in his family until a woman from Tekoa (2 Samuel 14:1–24) confronted David and challenged him to bring Absalom home. Absalom returned to Jerusalem, but he remained isolated from David for two full years. Moreover, the eventual contact between Absalom and his father was not initiated by David. That contact was initiated by Absalom, who created a crisis by setting Joab's field on fire as a means of getting his dad's attention!

Father and son did finally connect in a warm embrace (2 Samuel 14:33), but unfortunately it was a brief window of affection. Eventually, Absalom led a revolution against his own father. Whatever took place between David and Absalom was not significant or long-lasting enough to bring about permanent change in the father-son relationship.

Why didn't David do something to resolve the family sickness? He was a great warrior and leader, adored by his people. He was talented, gifted in music and poetry. He had been successful in defending his nation. As a teenager David had kept his country safe by killing the giant warrior Goliath. Yet the truth is that with all of his confidence and spirituality, David did not know how to deal with the conflict among his children. He did not know how to handle pain in any way other than avoidance and passivity.

What we need to learn is that even though David failed his family in this way, it doesn't mean he *wanted* to fail them: *He was doing the best he knew how to do.*

As parents we find it difficult to be and do toward our spouses and/or children what we have not experienced ourselves. In other words, our natural tendency is to repeat with our children what we experienced as kids.

So it behooves us to read, seek mentors, counselors, and wise friends, and to observe healthy families so we don't automatically repeat a destructive pattern simply because it "feels familiar."

David was most likely passing on the dysfunction he "inherited" from his family of origin to his own kids. There's an old saying that if one person heals, it heals many generations. Imagine the power you have to turn the tide of painful patterns and leave a legacy of health and wholeness for your children and generations to come.

3. *Time does* not *"heal all wounds" when it comes to family issues.*
Two brothers who had once been close went to hear their father's will read after their dad had died. To their shock, the father had left all the assets of the family business to the older brother. The younger brother received nothing. The brothers argued ferociously over the outcome of the will, but the older brother refused to share the assets that were more important to him than the relationship.

A canyon of bitterness opened between the brothers. The two brothers have children who are middle-aged. Now even these cousins share the "inheritance" of family bitterness—all because two adults could not find a way to reconcile.

That must have been what Absalom experienced during the seven years before finally having the chance to hug his father, King David, again. He had tried, in various destructive ways, to get the "I need attention!" message across. But no one detected his deeper need. As time progressed, his anger and hurt must have turned into a well of rage that overflowed in the revolution he led against his father. The decisions Absalom made led to a grisly death: Joab took three spears and thrust them through his heart (2 Samuel 18:14). He died, most likely never knowing how his father truly felt about him. It was such a needless tragedy.

Even seven years after his estrangement from Absalom, David grieved over the loss of his son. In his grief it is apparent that he loved his son deeply: "The king was deeply moved and went up to the chamber over the gate and wept. And thus he said as he walked, 'O my son Absalom, my son, my son Absalom! Would I had died instead of you, O Absalom, my son, my son!'" (2 Samuel 18:33)

The pain and frustration of never having experienced a warm relationship with his son must have been excruciating, a deep hurt that only intensified with time. The adage "time heals all wounds" was not true in this case, and it rarely is in life today.

4. Change that happens inside needs to translate outwardly into relational changes.

The Bible calls David a "man after [God's own] heart" (Acts 13:22; see also 1 Samuel 13:14). His writings in the book of Psalms indicate that David was capable of deep feelings and emotions, at least when it came to his relationship to God. Moving expressions of the depth of his hurt, the grief and shame of his sin, and other emotions come leaping out of those pages.

David could work out emotionally difficult situations with God. Yet did that translate into improved relationships with his children? We have no evidence that his children knew or experienced the sensitive side of their father. Through his emotion-laden writings, we likely know more about David's vulnerable side than Amnon, Tamar, or Absalom did.

It is confusing when a family member has a spiritual side that seems active and real, but that spirituality or religious fervor doesn't translate into being more loving, kind, forgiving, and authentic within marital or parent/child interactions. The most effective way for us to share our faith with our kids or our friends is not to preach at them but to be Christlike to them. When our actions and words don't jibe with our "God talk," the stage is set for relational and spiritual dysfunction.

5. You can always start over and learn from your mistakes.

David seems to have had a different kind of relationship with his son Solomon. At the beginning of Proverbs 4 Solomon wrote, "I was a son to my father, tender and the only son in the sight of my mother, then he taught me and said to me, 'Let your heart hold fast my words . . . hear, my son, and accept my sayings and the years of your life will be many.'" It appears that David did a better job in sharing his faith with Solomon in a way that Solomon could hear and receive.

It is never too late to be the spouse or parent you've always wanted to be. I know of one woman who tried for years to be the perfect wife and mom, but in the process she came across as plastic and unreal. Then one day a crisis forced her to cross a threshold and take a hard look at herself, her childhood wounds, family patterns, and the perfect mask she'd been wearing for years. She proactively took steps to heal. She read some good books, went to a small support group, and spent a week at an intensive Christian counseling center in the mountains.

Over time, she began to relax and express herself more vulnerably. She also learned to listen to her husband and kids without lecturing or preaching or giving advice. Though her kids were now teens and young adults, they noticed the change in their mother. One day her son said, "Mom, you've changed. You are more real now. I just want you to know I feel closer to you now than I did all those years when I was a kid and you were trying so hard to be the perfect mom. I can be myself with you now and enjoy just hanging out."

My friend later shared, "It was the highest compliment I'd ever received from my kids! And all because I took a good look within and allowed God to teach me how to relax in who I am and quit worrying so much about being perfect at everything."

WHAT DOES IT TAKE FOR A FAMILY TO RECOVER?

There are six steps to help an individual or family in their journey toward wholeness.

1. Be Proactive

Take action. Take a step. Get into a support group where you can gather with other people who are dealing with similar problems. Read books about recovery and healing. Form a small group with other people who are committed to sharing honestly and openly, who are willing to support you when help is needed, and who are committed to praying for you—as you are for them. People who make big, positive changes that last are diligent and proactive with their healing.

If you respond passively in the face of difficult problems, what will be the results of that choice down the road? Consider Bill. No matter what Bill did, his wife got angry at him. He could never do enough to please her. Her moodiness was like a dark cloud over the whole family. Bill and the kids lived in a state of chronic tension, never knowing when a thunderbolt was going to strike or the next tornado might whirl through the family, leaving in its path destruction and wreckage of hearts and feelings.

When Bill began to realize that he could change only himself, he gave up trying to pacify his stormy wife. His men's support group gave him a place where he could be open about his hurt and frustration. When his wife was depressed and moody, he didn't try to "fix" her. He and the kids just left to go do fun things while she napped at home, depressed and angry.

Eventually, she realized that the family was going to go on without her and began to focus more on resolving her own issues. She saw the wisdom in facing the storm within herself rather than allowing depression and anger to spill out over the whole family. Thankfully, today the family no longer lives in a continuous rainy season—there are times of sunlight, soft clouds, and deep blue skies.

2. Be Prepared for This to Take Time

In today's fast-paced world, many of us want everything to happen yesterday. But healing from wounds takes time. Some hurts, angers, and traumas will not go away immediately. A woman or man who was the victim of incest as a child must deal not only with the hurt, anger, and betrayal connected with the molestation but also must totally restructure his or her self-image. He or she needs to resolve issues of sexuality, trust, and shame—in short, relearn how to deal with life in general.

As Christians it is easy to shame ourselves for taking too much time to get over a loss. But the truth is that healing deep hurt takes time. Healing is not something that can be rushed, no matter how hard we push ourselves. Not even our well-meaning Christian friends who chide us for taking a healthy amount of time to be okay can shorten the duration it takes to heal.

3. Absorb New Learning and Information

It is hard to know what "normal" is when you come from a dysfunctional family. If all you saw as you were growing up was fighting and chaos, how can you know how to resolve a conflict? How do you work through your anger? As a father, how do you emotionally connect with your wife and children if you never experienced sharing feelings in a healthy relationship with your own father? If all you knew as a child was sexual abuse, how can you automatically enjoy lovemaking as good and natural in marriage? If you have never seen good communication modeled, how are you supposed to model good communication with your own children and spouse?

Classes, books, call-in talk radio shows, blogs, mentors, therapists, seminars, podcasts, Scriptures, specially formulated "healing" Bible studies, weekend retreats, and 12-Step Programs/Support groups are just some of the sources people turn to when they are beginning to relearn how to deal with life and relationships in a healthy, balanced way. You might try reading some of the books listed in the appendix or start a discussion group using this book or other self-help books. There are many wonderful, twelve-week Bible studies available that focus around issues of healing from your past and moving forward in freedom. Seek out a mentor who is empathetic to your past and present but is further along in his or her journey toward wholeness.

There are other resources all around you. Ask for help. Don't pretend to know everything. We have all learned to fake confidence, even when deep down we are scared and uncertain. Yet most times help is available for the asking.

The point is: You need to reprogram your mind with new information. That may be obvious advice, but it is a critical step in recovery.

4. Do *Whatever It Takes*

If you have a mountain to overcome, develop the attitude that you will make a way to do it: climbing over the mountain, tunneling through it, walking around it, or hiring a hot air balloon to float your way over it. There is no easy way out—no magic fix. Perseverance will pay off when you set your mind toward getting emotionally well and doing all you can to help your family do the same. Remember that just one person, healed, can affect not only your own family but also the generations to come. There's no greater task to take on!

Doing what it takes means abandoning the excuses you've been using for not getting better. You can't let excuses confine you in your pain. You may need to make room in your already busy schedule for regular 12-step groups. You may need to swallow some pride and go to a trusted friend, pastor, mentor, or therapist and say, "I need help. Can you meet with me on a regular basis for awhile?"

Adopting the determination to do *whatever it takes* to recover makes all the difference between those who get better and those who give up and go back to old unhealthy ways. Passivity and inactivity will only bring you more trouble, usually in the form of prolonged agony.

5. Dump Your Shame

Often a beginning place to healing is to dump what is not working for us. Chapter 5 of this book is devoted to the subject of shame, but it bears brief mention here, too.

Family shame, cultural shame, and religious shame are emotionally deadly. Put briefly, shame is false guilt. It is the pervasive sense that "I am defective, inadequate, and worthless as a person." Shame is typically piled on us by others, not by God. It is different from normal healthy guilt that leads us to confess, repent, and make amends. Shame is insidious and feels unremovable, like a permanent part of our psyche. It takes work to move from a shame-based family system to one that respects and honors people in the family. In some cultures where shame is used to manipulate obedience even from adults, it takes time to sort out the difference between respecting elders, for example, without allowing them to rule your life. When you grow up in a culture, that culture provides the only system that you know, so it is especially tricky to see without outside help what is healthy about that culture vs. what is shame-based in it.

The route out of shame is honor, respect, and affirmation of all family members. For example, in many families and churches the only time women are honored and respected is on Mother's Day. The rest of the year, women are relegated to back-of-the-bus status in terms of honor and respect. If a child grows up never seeing his father respect, affirm, and value his mother (or vice versa), he too will devalue the other sex. In fact, most abusive men saw this attitude modeled by some other significant male mentor in their lives, usually their father.

It often takes a great deal of new information and learning before a person can get hold of the shaming experiences in his family of origin, ethnic culture, or religious background and can begin to treat himself and the people around him differently.

6. Develop a Committed and Genuine Spirituality

No authentic and long-lasting change occurs without God's help and the work of the Holy Spirit in a person's life. A committed and genuine spirituality is an essential foundation for recovery.

Let's face it: Most real change in our attitudes is the result of God's grace in our lives. But we have a responsibility to be sold out to following Him, especially during recovery. When the heat is on, as it often is when you are trying to forsake old patterns and adopt new ones, your commitment to healthy emotional choices will be truly tested. No formula for recovery is complete without God's help.

Jesus said, "I am the vine, you are the branches; he who abides in Me and I in him, he bears much fruit, for apart from Me you can do nothing" (John 15:5). To "abide in Him" means to settle down and make our home in Him, which conveys an element of love and trust that is real and natural, and also daily and consistent.

We can be honest with God, no matter how messed up our lives are. Read the psalms, and see the honesty of the emotions expressed there. Read the Gospels, and see Jesus' honest reactions to emotionally charged situations. It's often hard for those who've not had healthy, kind parents to believe that God will treat them fairly. However, God deals with all his children as a compassionate Father and a faithful friend.

HEALING AND RECOVERY

There is great hope: God desires our healing, and He is able to bring it about. That is the focus of this book.

Over the years, I've seen God make powerful use of 12-step programs as tools of healing. At first when people attend such meetings they may be unimpressed, since the gatherings are often relatively unstructured and not exactly glitzy productions. As they stay and listen, though, people begin to marvel at the honesty and the absence of judgmental attitudes in the meetings.

Many people experience for the first time the power of God's love and caring through the acceptance and honesty in a typical meeting. Tim was one such young man. His mother tried her best to get him to go to church with her, but the harder she tried, the more he resisted. Sound familiar? If you are the parent of a strong-willed teen, it probably does.

Tim finally hit rock bottom. It dawned on him that drug use was ruining his life. He'd already dropped out of high school, and he knew college would be out of the question if something didn't change. He began attending a 12-step group and through simple prayer asked God to help him to stay sober one day at a time. Amazed, Tim found that prayer helped! His sobriety, too, now allowed him to think clearly for the first time in many years.

He decided to attend a church service with his mother. During the service Tim prayed to receive the gift of grace that Christ offered. Tim first began to experience God's power through the 12-step program. God used that program to help him find a Savior. Today Tim has a deeply rooted, genuine, and committed spirituality that continues to bring wanted changes to his life.

So have hope! Emotional and relational healing is indeed available. In fact, King David's entire life was one of recovery from one terrible mistake or sin after another! And we are talking *major* stuff here: adultery, murder, blowing it as a parent. It isn't the mistakes we make that define our lives as much as the lessons we glean from those mistakes. Perhaps this is one of the reasons that, in spite of his checkered past, David is known as a man after God's heart.

Be encouraged that God is always delighted to meet you where you are, but He will never leave you there. He will work with you patiently to bring you to a better place, just as He loved and worked with David.

Questions for Reflection

1. As we can see in the lives of David's adult children, time by itself does not heal all wounds. What issues have you put off, hoping that time would change them? What relationships have you been avoiding taking steps to improve? Make a short list of the issues you might address with God's help.

2. David was honest in his relationship with God, yet he had trouble allowing those relationship skills to translate into improvements in his dealings with his children. What are some risks and steps you can take in your relationships with your children, whether they are young or adults?

3. David's life was not defined by his mistakes but rather by what he learned from his mistakes and the way he continued to get up and seek God's help and grace. Make a list of some of the sins or mistakes you have made in the past and the lessons that you learned from them and perhaps how you've applied those lessons to avoid further mistakes.

2

Isaac and His Family Tree

Dave Carder

WHAT COMES to mind when you read the following description: an only child born late in life to wealthy parents who had an overwhelming need for a male heir? Likely the word *spoiled*.

Isaac was his name. His birth was remarkable. Over many years and on multiple occasions God had given His word to Abraham, Isaac's father, that he should have descendants (Genesis 12:2, 7; 15:1–21), but decades went by and Abraham's wife, Sarah, was still barren. Then, when Sarah was eighty-nine and Abraham ninety-nine, there came a more specific word: "My covenant I will establish with Isaac, whom Sarah will bear to you at this season next year" (17:21; see also 18:14). So when Isaac was born he was more than just the long-awaited fulfillment of a promise: He was a miracle child.

But Isaac also represented a problem. Many years earlier, out of desperation for an heir, Sarah, apparently following a cultural pattern, had offered her personal servant, Hagar, to Abraham as surrogate to bear a son in her name. From that union had come Ishmael (16:1–16). Hagar's pregnancy created severe dissension in Abraham's household (16:1–16), and only the Lord's direct intervention made it possible for Hagar to remain (16:7–12).

Now Isaac's birth rekindled old animosities. "Drive out this maid and her son," Sarah raged at Abraham, "for the son of this maid shall not be an heir with my son Isaac" (21:10). Isaac's birth had created what today we would call a blended family: Hagar, Ishmael, Abraham, Sarah, and Isaac; and there could be no family peace unless someone gave way. The dynamics already present in Isaac's family when he was born and incidents that occurred as he was growing up had a profound impact on his life and are part of the reason why a chapter in this book is devoted to him. For though Isaac was a link in a chain of descendants that would reach all the way to the Lord Jesus Christ, he was not immune from dysfunctional influences brought to bear by his family of origin and family tree. Just as they would for you or me, those influences helped make Isaac what he became.

As we examine the emotional dynamics that influenced Isaac's life, let me emphasize that the goal is not to criticize Isaac. Throughout the Old Testament Jehovah cited His special love for His people by describing Himself as "the God of Abraham, Isaac, and Jacob," and Jesus Himself used the expression (Matthew 22:32; Mark 12:26; Luke 20:37). Abraham's trust in God is referred to in Romans 4, Hebrews 11, and James 2 as the epitome of faith, and all of the patriarchs are cited in the roll call of saints found in Hebrews 11 (vv. 17, 20–21).

Moreover, all three of the patriarchs were the special objects of God's love. In Genesis 22:16–18 God says to Abraham, "Because you have . . . not withheld your son, your only son, indeed I will greatly bless you. . . . In your seed all the nations of the earth shall be blessed, because you have obeyed My voice." The Lord gave similar blessings to Isaac and Jacob years later in separate incidents:

> I am the God of your father Abraham; Do not fear, for I am with you. I will bless you, and multiply your descendants, for the sake of My servant Abraham. (26:24)
>
> I am the Lord, the God of your father Abraham and the God of Isaac; the land on which you lie, I will give it to you and your descendants. . . . Behold, I am with you and will keep you wherever you go, and will bring you back to this land; for I will not leave you until I have done what I have promised you. (28:13–15)

So Abraham, Isaac, and Jacob had a special, unique relationship to God. But there are two sides to Isaac's life. One side reflects his walk with and obedience to God. The other side, the one on which this chapter will focus, reflects the sometimes troubled interpersonal relationships that existed among the members of Isaac's family. Again, this is not to suggest that the patriarchs were afflicted by some sort of Jekyll-Hyde personality disorder or that they habitually said one thing while doing the other. Quite to the contrary; each truly had a heart for God. But, like you and me, the patriarchs were humanly flawed, and we can learn something from those flaws.

The patriarchs were the products of their own families of origin and of the everyday situations they encountered. They struggled regularly with their emotions and in their relationships. Real life, both then and now, is difficult. On this planet it has always been that way and will continue to be so until Jesus establishes the new heaven and new earth (see Genesis 3:17–19).

If any of the material in this chapter sounds far-fetched or too strongly steeped in twenty-first-century thinking, remember that the goal is to understand the emotional dynamics at work at an important juncture in Isaac's life. If you can take away the "spiritualizing" about the patriarchs you have heard for years and put yourself in Isaac's state of mind, you will begin to understand at a personal level some of the remarkable events chronicled in the book of Genesis.

BEING SPECIAL OFTEN MAKES BEING "REAL" VERY DIFFICULT

The biographer of the patriarchs does not always tell his story from exactly the same perspective. Sometimes he gives an inside look at the personal struggles the patriarchs experienced. At other times he steps back and allows the reader to draw his own conclusions from the circumstances he presents. Yet always he presents the patriarchs as real people pursuing their walk with God with admirable wholeheartedness. Keep that in mind as you read the discussion in this chapter of the personal side of the relationships and family styles of the patriarchs.

Let's briefly run though a checklist of what the family had to deal with. There was a *father*, Abraham, who was desperate for an heir; a *mother,*

Sarah, whose identity was wrapped up in the cultural purpose of producing a male child; a *half-brother*, Ishmael, who was despised; a *blended family* in which Isaac was the favored child; an *overly close (fused) relationship* between Sarah and Isaac that produced dependency; a *traumatic experience* between Isaac and his father, Abraham, at the altar of sacrifice at Mt. Moriah; and an *immense inheritance* that Isaac had no part in developing. If one looks at just these basic facts, it is apparent that Isaac grew up in a family with many of the same negative influences that affect our own families. That circumstance should not be surprising. Families are complex systems, whether set in the twenty-first century or millennia before the time of Christ.

ISAAC'S NEAR-DEATH EXPERIENCE

To better understand Isaac's family system, let's look at the patriarchal family tree from Abraham to Jacob. Keep in mind that, just as it is difficult for us to sort out all the influences that have shaped our development, so also it is difficult to identify all the factors that shaped Isaac's personal history. Assessing Isaac's case is made even more difficult by the cultural difference we need to bridge in reading about him, the lapse in time from his to ours, and the sketchiness of the Genesis history. Many details of the story we would like to know about are not addressed. Nevertheless, one event stands out as overwhelmingly influential in Isaac's formative years: his near-sacrifice on Mt. Moriah at the hands of his father, Abraham.

That experience must have been a turning point in Isaac's life, the kind of experience a person never forgets and from which point his life is forever different. The background we have already mentioned: Isaac is the favorite child in the family; he has virtually no sibling competition; he alone will inherit his father's wealth; he has been trained all of his life to care for his father's business. In short, he has been prepared for life as an "only son of royalty."

As one reads the Mt. Moriah passage in Genesis 22, Isaac's growing apprehension of what is to come stands out. He asks his father, "My father! . . . Behold, the fire and the wood, but where is the lamb for the burnt offering?" (22:7). He must have been puzzled by Abraham's vague answer

("God will provide"), but nevertheless Isaac continued with his father up the mountain. He further submitted to his father amidst mounting fears as his father bound him and laid him upon the altar. Isaac by this time surely would have been strong enough to resist, so his cooperation in being bound demonstrates great respect for his father. Still, it is safe to say that as he lay down upon the altar he experienced mixed emotions about what was taking place.

While bound and lying upon the altar, Isaac must have felt overwhelming confusion as he realized that he was the sacrifice. Just as we would, he surely must have struggled with terror at the sight of his father raising a knife above his chest, preparing to plunge it into his heart.

What trauma! Put yourself in Isaac's place: Feel the wood on *your* back, the cords on *your* wrists. In your mind's eye, have your father stand in the place of Abraham and think about the knife entering your body. Your thoughts and feelings would have to be magnified one-hundredfold for you truly to understand what Isaac went through there.

Trauma reshapes a person's life. People are thoroughly different afterward. Survivors become more cautious, often less trusting, and at the very least more aware of their immediate environment. Recovering victims of trauma, especially when loved ones were involved, will tell you that values such as security, safety, attachment, and predictability become all-important to them. Being human, Isaac would have shared that normal response to trauma.

Possibly you are struggling with the question, Why did this have to happen to Isaac? It seems unfair that Isaac had to experience so traumatic an event. Thinking people through the centuries have wrestled with this Old Testament story, and those of us who hold to the inerrancy of Scripture still need to exercise faith as we cling to Hebrews 11:17: "By faith Abraham, when he was tested, offered up Isaac . . . "

But the question under discussion in this section of the chapter has not to do with why but rather with how. It is not why God set up this test of faith for Abraham but rather how that test of faith affected Isaac. Don't mix the two. The event on Mt. Moriah was Abraham's great test of faith, and his faithful follow-through placed him in faith's hall of fame (Hebrews

11). The fallout in Isaac's life, however, was somewhat different, and that is the subject of this chapter.

This discussion could be had regarding nearly all of the Christian martyrs throughout Christian history, as well as virtually all of the survivors of any modern-day trauma: Though we think first of the martyrs themselves, the ones left alive often suffer the most.

THE TRAUMA REPEATED

In counseling victims of sexual and physical abuse, one result that often emerges is their post-trauma struggle to trust others because of their fear that they could again be taken advantage of. It is the consequence of the normal human questions: *Why would you do this to me? What did I do to deserve this?*

Since Isaac was human, given the Mt. Moriah experience he naturally would struggle with the concepts of faith and trust. It would be difficult for him to find himself in a place of risk that exposed him to the danger that others might take advantage of him. He would be especially sensitive to the feeling of being deceived or tricked. People who have been abandoned often fear abandonment when none is intended, and Isaac's response to the event on Mt. Moriah would have led to a similar hypersensitivity regarding issues of deception.

To be sure, Abraham on Mt. Moriah didn't intend to deceive his son. He was simply "following orders" from on high. But it is reasonable to suggest that Isaac, while under the knife, may have felt he had been deceived. After all, on the way up the mountain he had specifically asked his father about the missing sacrificial lamb and had received an answer, albeit a puzzling one. It was not until later, on the way down the mountain, that his father could have filled him in on all the details, including the fact that God had directly set into motion this test of faith.

Isaac's sensitivity to deceit, experienced early in life, probably formed the basis many years later for Isaac's intense emotional reaction (trembling) to his son Jacob's trickery in obtaining the birthright and the blessing (Genesis 27:33). The conditions of the earlier event on Mt. Moriah have an ironic relationship to the conditions in place when Jacob seeks his father's blessing. In the experience at Moriah, Isaac could see what was happening ("Father, where's the lamb?"), but his innocent heart could not envision that he would be the sacrifice. When he is old and wise with experience he is blind and cannot see what is occurring (Genesis 27:21–29). Earlier, with his father Abraham, Isaac could see what was happening but could not comprehend it. Later, with his son Jacob, he can comprehend that things are not right but cannot see to verify it. The second experience calls forth the pain of the first experience, and Isaac "trembled violently" (Genesis 27:33), experiencing the combined pain of both deeply felt experiences.

EMOTIONALLY SEPARATED FROM HIS FATHER ABRAHAM

Many years earlier, Abraham had shown genuine concern for Hagar and Ishmael when Sarah had demanded he banish them to the desert (21:9–13). So intense were Abraham's feelings of divided loyalty that God Himself had to comfort him. Most of us as parents can relate to Abraham's experience of feeling torn apart trying to keep estranged individuals (in this case, Hagar and Sarah) happy with us and with each other. Abraham's response to the tension between Hagar and Sarah, the heartfelt hospitality he showed to strangers, and his burdened intercession for Lot and his family in Sodom and Gomorrah provide a picture of a man who is self-sacrificing, compassionate, and extremely loyal (Genesis 18).

But when it came to Abraham's daily relationships with those people one might think would matter most, the people in his immediate family, a different picture emerges. Just as we do, Abraham had a dark side to his relationships with those in his family tree. For much of his life he was physically and emotionally separated from his kin. Called of God, Abraham left his family of origin in Haran with no biblical record of his ever returning (12:1), even though it was only seven days' journey away (31:23). He was adamant that even Isaac should never return to Haran (Genesis 24:5–8). Though evidently Abraham regarded it as a good place to find a wife (both Abraham and Isaac chose wives for their sons from the family of Bethuel), he did not regard it as a good place to visit. Sounds a lot like our current in-law family settings, doesn't it?

Earlier, Abraham had separated from his nephew Lot (13:8–11), with whom he had traveled, nomad-style, for years. Eventually he even gave up Sarah, denying (lying) that she was his wife (20:1–18). This abandonment by denial was the more significant because God had already told Abraham that Sarah would bear him a son in the not-too-distant future (17:16).

In his symbolic abandonment of his family, Abraham revealed himself to be more like us than we would like to admit. When it comes right down to it, all of us have a tendency to be self-serving and self-protective. Many marital and family problems are maintained in family trees through self-serving and self-protective measures on the part of one or both parents. Such patterns often parallel Abraham's pattern of maintaining emotional separation from those inside the family while appearing to outsiders as loyal, compassionate, and sacrificing.

After Sarah's death, Abraham continued to distance himself from Isaac by producing an entirely different large family through Keturah, his new wife, and numerous concubines (25:1–6). To cap it off, Abraham died without, it seems, ever passing on a patriarchal blessing to his son Isaac.

ENMESHED WITH HIS MOTHER, SARAH

Because we do not live in a culture in which women receive their identity almost solely through producing a male child (see the story of Rachel and Leah, Genesis 29:1–30:24), it is nearly impossible for us to fully understand what happened to Sarah when she finally bore her only son at the age of ninety. Not only did she experience the joy of those around her, she experienced the internal joy of achieving at last what she was always supposed to be able to do. She had finally arrived. She had borne a son.

So Isaac was doubly important to Sarah. He was important to her because her identity was excessively tied to producing a male child (16:1–6) and because he was her one and only chance at motherhood. Isaac was her "miracle baby." Today, any woman struggling with infertility who finally conceives and bears a son, the only one she can ever have, can relate to the emotions Sarah experienced. The natural protectiveness Sarah would have had toward Isaac, the pride she would feel, would have been indescribable. In a real sense, from her point of view, Isaac *belonged* to Sarah.

Sarah loved Isaac, maybe too much. She needed him, probably too much. The emotionally charged atmosphere of this mother-son relation-ship is alluded to at Sarah's death (24:67): Abraham, the husband who had been married to her for more than one hundred years, grieved for the normal period of bereavement, but not Isaac. Sarah died when Isaac was thirty-seven (17:17; 23:1). At forty, *three years* after she was gone, when he married Rebekah (24:67; 25:20), he was still grieving. This enmeshment (a concept more fully discussed in chapter 8), in the mother-son relationship of Isaac and Sarah helped set the stage for the later emotional separation of Isaac from Rebekah.

EMOTIONALLY DISTANT FROM HIS WIFE REBEKAH

Those who work with divorce and remarriage indicate that a second mar-riage is usually doomed if it follows too closely on the heels of the former one. The second marriage is commonly referred to as a "rebound relation-ship," an attempt to heal the pain of the loss of the previous relationship by becoming involved in a new one. The dynamics of a rebound relation-ship were at work in the marriage of Isaac and Rebekah.

Isaac's marriage was arranged by Abraham. Abraham, aware of how keenly Isaac felt the loss of his mother and probably trying to be helpful, decided to care for Isaac by finding him a wife. Perhaps there had not been room in Isaac's life for a wife while his mother was still alive. Relationships that are too close emotionally, i.e., that are *fused* or *enmeshed*, characteris-tically cut other individuals completely out of the picture. But, in Isaac's case, Mom was gone, and marriage appeared to be a route to solace and comfort. Of course, we know that marriage as a substitute for the love of a deceased mother is only destined for pain and frustration (ask any woman who has married her mother-in-law's favorite only son), but Isaac—and Abraham—did not know that, and Abraham's servant was sent to Abra-ham's home country to find a wife for Isaac.

Often individuals who are "stuck" in the grieving process will not change the environment the deceased person created. They keep the same living arrangements, drive the same car, and wear the same clothes as though the lost loved one were still present. It is easy to imagine that Isaac kept the tent exactly as his mother left it. After all, he had become accustomed to his mother's care and nurture for thirty-seven years. Sarah was probably the most important woman in his life.

This loss of his mother, taken together with having an emotionally distant father, coupled with the trauma experienced at the altar on Mt. Moriah, left Isaac all alone. His separation was made more intense by his father's decision to remarry (Genesis 25:1). That produced another blended family! Over the next thirty-eight years Abraham fathered at least six more sons (Genesis 25:2–6).

It is easy to imagine that, at first, marriage to Rebekah was an intense bonding experience. Isaac was lonely and grieving; Rebekah was completely cut off from her family. Initially they needed each other desperately. It was not long, however, before the unfinished business in the relationship of Isaac and his mother became apparent.

Rebekah soon realized that she needed to become "another Sarah" to Isaac. As she struggled with her relationship to Isaac and with Isaac's relationship to his mother, her own identity began to disappear. In a culture where women's opinions did not really matter, Rebekah would have had to keep her frustrations bottled up inside. Along with her failure to become pregnant, Rebekah must have struggled with terrible feelings of inadequacy for the next twenty years (25:20–26). The one thing that she could do for Isaac as his wife—something Sarah, as his mother, could never do—was to provide him with children, and she was failing even in that.

The relief of finally becoming pregnant with Jacob and Esau must have been overwhelming for Rebekah. How she must have anticipated the joy of finally being fully appreciated for who she was, after providing the much longed-for sons. She must have thought, *Now that I have brought forth sons, my husband and I can focus on our relationship*. Imagine her pain and disappointment when Isaac chose instead to love one of the children, Esau—and the wrong one at that (25:28)! Rebekah found herself with no one else but Jacob. Instead of focusing on each other, she and Isaac each chose a son to love.

At his marriage, at the birth of his children, and finally at one of Rebekah's most difficult moments, Isaac continued to "abandon" his wife. When he was faced with possible death because of Rebekah's beauty, Isaac denied their marital relationship to King Abimelech (26:6–11). His sons, Jacob and Esau, had to have seen this abandonment through denial, for they were young men at the time. Through modeling, Isaac was adversely shaping his sons' attitudes toward women.

Where did Isaac get the idea of abandoning Rebekah? Was it just a common cultural practice? Did it come with his genes? My hypothesis is that Sarah, in her inappropriately close relationship to her son Isaac, at some point told him about the time Abraham had abandoned her to this very same Abimelech (Genesis 20). Even though he must surely have despised Abraham's tactics, Isaac was not above practicing them with his own spouse. A pattern of pain is likely to be passed down the line unless something concrete is done to interrupt it.

DESPISING WHAT SHOULD BE VALUED

In both families, parents and children were learning to despise what is important. Isaac gave up his wife just after Esau actually gave up his birthright. Isaac's abandonment of his wife provided the groundwork for her mistrust of him. She could see that she did not always count with her husband. When the chips were down, Isaac would place his security over hers. That concept, coupled with Isaac's attachment to Esau, pushed her later into taking matters into her own hands; if she could only get the inheritance for her son Jacob, Rebekah's future would be secure. Surely her boy Jacob would take care of her all her life, even if her husband wouldn't.

This devaluing of what is important almost always underlies the development of family secrets, as well as contributing to dependency (addictions and compulsive behavior) and codependency (the need to have someone in the family responsible for another's irresponsibility). During the rest of this book, we'll examine these and related topics.

ENMESHED WITH HIS SON ESAU, THE ONE WHOM GOD REJECTED

Why would Isaac, himself the promised child—a type of Christ in the Old Testament—turn from the child God chose, Jacob, in favor of Esau? Was it only due to his taste for wild game (25:28)? Though that certainly played a part in Isaac's choice, there were also other factors at work.

First, Esau had a bent to be and do all that Isaac had never been able to be and do. Here was a chance for Isaac to become vicariously "a man's man." Here was the opportunity for this "mama's boy" to become a hunter through his son's excellent skills. Now he could feel what it was like to take risks. Now he could move out from under the smothering protection of being the "only" and favorite son. Now perhaps he could develop some self-identity through his son's achievement. After all, wasn't he Esau's father?

The favoritism Isaac showed toward Esau was probably initially simple fatherly pride in his son's achievements. That is normal for any dad. But it got out of hand when Isaac decided to bequeath the blessing differently from what God decreed (25:23). Isaac was never overtly angry and was typically fearful of confrontation (see 26:18–22, where Isaac withdraws from several contested wells and digs new ones as opposed to standing up for what rightfully belongs to him). It was in keeping with Isaac's personality and the culture of the time for him to extend the blessing to the son he thought stood before him, his elder son, Esau, even though he well knew that such a blessing was contrary to explicit prophecy given before the sons were born (25:23).

Favoritism in a family is common. And, contrary to the opinion many people have, I think that as long as it does not lead to unjust treatment of the children, favoritism is not by itself wrong. Almost every family has a favorite child. That does not mean the parents love that child more than they love their other children. It only means that the favorite child *fits* better with the personality of the parents. They often see things alike or have shared interests that tie them together.

Jesus had favorites even among His disciples. The special three are well known for the times they alone shared with the Savior (Peter, James, and John in Gethsemane, Matthew 26:36–37; and at the Transfiguration, 17:1–8). Among that select group, John stood closer to Jesus than the others (John 13:23–25; 21:20). Jesus didn't love John more than Peter; He just loved him differently. He and John fit together better. In the vernacular of our day, they were "on the same wavelength."

But it was more than favoritism that Esau and Jacob faced at the giving of the blessing. On a spiritual level, the birthright given to the younger son reflected God's will that the family line should continue through Jacob and not Esau. On a personal level, the giving of the birthright involved intense competition for parental approval. Even after Jacob had stolen the birthright through deception, Esau still struggled to regain his parents' favor by marrying a woman of whom his parents approved (Genesis 28:6–9; cf. 26:35; 27:46).

In the passing of the blessing, we see unfinished business, a family's secret that goes undiscussed and unaddressed until it flowers into the open. As a result, Jacob leaves the family, terrified (Genesis 27:42–45), and Esau leaves it angry and bitter, with plans in his heart to murder (27:41).

ISAAC SEPARATED FROM HIS SON JACOB

If we can step back and look again at the relationship of Isaac and his sons when the boys were young, we can see a negative pattern in the interaction of the family members. In keeping with the culture, Isaac preferred the elder son to receive the family blessing. He relegated Jacob, as the second born, to his mother to raise. As a result, the first picture we have of Jacob in the Scriptures is cooking food within the family compound (25:27–29). The arrangement sets up an exact replay of Isaac's own family experience.

Interestingly, we do not ever see Jacob express remorse over taking advantage of his father's old age and lying to him. After all, wasn't it his mother who had protected him all of his life? Hadn't she always been the one to whom he went when he was injured or in need? Knowing he was "the special one," Rebekah surely must have told her favorite son that God had chosen him. As mothers often do to reassure children, she most likely inadvertently played into the pattern by repeatedly telling Jacob the story of his birth and selection by God.

The rejection Jacob experienced when his father favored Esau would only intensify his questions and deepen his pain. *If Jehovah is the God of my father and Jehovah has chosen me, why has my father rejected me?* he might have asked himself and his mother. *If God's plan is going to be fulfilled,* he must have thought, *my mother and I must cooperate in treachery.* Though she surely did not consciously want to do so, Rebekah's actions and advice in the matter of the birthright must have conveyed the view that God cannot be trusted to do what He says He will do (i.e., give Jacob the blessing). She ended up modeling mistrust of God—the exact opposite of the attitude she wanted Jacob to have as an adult.

Looking at this situation from a family systems view, as long as each child had a parent sympathetic with and partial to him, equilibrium in the family was maintained. It was only when Jacob was able to deceive Isaac and steal the birthright from Esau that the balance of power shifted in the family. Now Jacob had both parents on his side. Esau was cut off. Sibling rivalry soared to thoughts of premeditated murder. Throughout the period prior to the power shift, the family would have appeared to be normal. Things looked so good on the outside that no one would have suspected that the underlying dynamics that would rip the family apart were already in place. For a while, it worked. As long as everyone stayed in his role, performed his task, and carried out his life assignment, all was well. But the family structure was rigid and, as a result, fragile. When pressure came, as it inevitably does, the family shattered.

Not only did Rebekah not trust Esau, but Esau came to despise Rebekah when he realized she was behind his brother's treachery. Jacob's and Esau's sibling rivalry brought to light rivalry that had existed between the parents for forty years. It was an undercover secret certainly, yet it was a powerful secret in a family that appeared—from the outside at least—to be at peace. How the dysfunction present in Isaac's family was maintained and handed from generation to generation will be discussed fully in a later chapter, which examines just how patterns are passed down a family tree.

Questions for Reflection

1. What "religious experiences" did you have as a child or an adolescent that have influenced your relationship with God? Have you ever been able to talk about those experiences with anyone?

2. Who was the favorite child in your family? What differences in treatment did the favorite receive?

3. If you are a parent, who is your favorite child and why?

4. What kind of inappropriate relationships exist in your immediate family history (grandparents, parents)? Who was inappropriately close? Who was withdrawn when it should have been the other way around? What impact have these relationships had on you, your relationship to your spouse, and your relationship with God?

5. How do you feel as you read about and think about dysfunction in the family systems of the patriarchs? What have you learned? What concepts can you apply to your own family tree?

3

Jesus Had Family Issues, Too

Earl Henslin

THEOLOGIANS CALL IT the mystery of the incarnation. We ordinary Christians call it both wonderful and puzzling. Wonderful in that Jesus shed His heavenly glory and came to earth to accomplish salvation; puzzling because it is hard to reconcile the homely details of Jesus' thirty-three years on earth with His majesty as holy God. Oh sure, we can glibly say that God dwelt on earth for a relatively short time in a human body, but what exactly did that look like?

The difference between biography and memoir is that biography provides a detailed chronological history of the author's life; memoir, however, just hits on the highlights, those transitional moments that helped form the personality of the subject. In some ways, what the Scriptures tell us about Jesus are like memoir in that they hit just a few of His major life stories from birth until death.

What we can deduce from these stories is that Jesus was both fully human and fully God. We know He experienced the whole range of human emotion, complete with temptation, yet never gave in to sin (Hebrews 4:15). We know Jesus had a divine Father and a human mother. And we know He grew up into adulthood in a mortal family that must have been very much like yours and mine. In summary, we are told that in Jesus' transition from boyhood to manhood he "kept increasing in wisdom and stature, and in favor with God and men." And yet those transitional years caused His parents at least one or two moments of real worry. If the parents of the Messiah struggled to let Him grow up and be independent, is there any doubt that almost all families have some difficulties in that transition period from childhood to teen years to adulthood?

In this chapter we are going to look at the sharp contrast between how the human members of Jesus' family of origin reacted to a couple of significant transitional moments and how the perfect Son of God reacted to them. We will see how Jesus resisted the pull toward dysfunctional relationships and behavior, even while people around Him, in their humanity, succumbed at times. In Jesus' living example we have a clear-cut pattern to follow in relating to others in the most healthy and functional ways possible.

JESUS' FIRST MIRACLE

The wedding at Cana is a favorite story of many Christians. If you can, take the time to reread the story in John 2:1–11, paying special attention to the family dynamics as the story unfolds.

Jesus and His disciples were invited to a wedding, where His mother was also in attendance. Weddings in those days lasted three days with feasting and wine. Apparently, however, the wine supply ran dry on the third day. So Mary said to her son, "They have no more wine." Jesus' answer is really interesting. "Dear woman, that's not our problem," Jesus replied. "My time has not yet come" (John 2:3–4 NLT).

These powerful words were spoken by Jesus directly, honestly, and respectfully to His mother. What did Jesus mean when He said them?

Observe again the context. Mary recognized the situation and wanted to help. She somehow knew her son could take care of the problem (which makes you wonder what sort of "miracles" she might have seen Him perform in their own backyard through the years), so she asked for help. However, note that she didn't really ask; instead, she sort of hinted: "They have no more wine." Instead of just coming right out and asking if He would do them a favor, she used what may have been a form of guilt motivation (i.e., "they're out of wine, you *should* help them"). Instead of forthrightly and honestly asking her son if He could help out, she "suggested" what He really "ought" to do.

Do you know anyone who acts like that? Perhaps you act like that. Yet it's much more healthy to ask a person flat-out to do you a favor instead of hinting around, expecting that person to pick up on what "obviously" is the "correct" response. Therapists often refer to this as a passive-aggressive style of communication.

Jesus responded strongly, clearly, and directly. He let His mother know His true feelings about her suggestions, expressing concern over the timing of going public with His ministry. Once a miracle was out of the bag in public, so to speak, there would be no turning back. Jesus would be, basically, announcing to the world that he was the Messiah. As the Son of God, Jesus must have felt this was a delicate matter that ought to be between Him and His heavenly Father, not between Him and His mother.

But then, for some unexplained reason (very possibly He was just showing His characteristic graciousness), Jesus went ahead and changed the water to wine. (Or perhaps His Father provided an inner "go-ahead," communicating to Him privately that indeed, now would be a fine time to proceed.) Whatever His inner motivation, Jesus decided to comply. He didn't do it out of obedience to His mother, for by now He was an adult (approximately thirty years old) and could decide for Himself. However, He may have chosen to do this out of love and respect for her. There is a huge difference here between an adult's knee-jerk obedience to parents and deferring to or honoring our parents by choice in specific incidences.

Because we cannot see the looks on the faces of Jesus and His mother, I am imagining one way of looking at this scenario. Some scholars believe there was actually some good-natured, mother-son teasing going on here, complete with winks and grins.

In an almost humorous—but all too human—turn of events, Mary seemed to ignore Jesus' words, turned instead to the servants, and said, "Do whatever he tells you." She assumed a lot about her son. She doesn't specifically know what He will do, but she does know her son's character, that He would do something, and it would be the right thing. Nevertheless, Mary does come off looking like a pushy mother, and perhaps she was. Rest assured, though, that Jesus was beyond being coerced, but not beyond responding to His very human mother in a way that would probably surprise even her. And Jesus used the situation to bring glory to God to boot. In fact, the final verse of the passage (v. 11) indicates that Jesus used the miracle of turning water into wine to build the faith of His disciples in His divine role on earth. "This miraculous sign at Cana in Galilee was the first time Jesus revealed his glory. And his disciples believed in him" (NLT).

Don't you love how Jesus used this homey, family opportunity to communicate deeper truths? His parables would later follow that pattern: using whatever situation was at hand to communicate a spiritual lesson.

The transition from child to teen, then adult is rarely easy and smooth for the adult child or parent. It takes time for parents to recognize that their kids have reached adulthood, with their own thoughts and plans that deserve respect. In healthy families, however, this transition is accomplished in a reasonable amount of time, with adult children standing up in a kind, mature, and reasonable way for their independence and with parents recognizing the time has come to let their adult children fly, or flail, or fall—allowing them the courtesy of living independently the life that they gave them.

Dysfunctional parents tend to force their own hidden agendas upon their children, even when those children have become adults. In homes like these, children were often raised to meet the emotional needs of their parents, instead of the healthy reverse. This pattern of expecting their adult children to continue to put their mom or dad first—above themselves and their wives and kids—is a common red flag signaling trouble. And if the problem pattern is not faced, adults can live a lifetime in bondage to their parents.

One example of this kind of adult bondage is Rod. He was married, had small children, was a hard-working man, and was well liked in general. Yet his wife was continually angry at him. As a "nice guy" Rod had a hard time accepting his part in the relational troubles. But with some help from a wise spiritual mentor, he began to see that, in truth, he was more emotionally married to his parents than he was to his wife. Because he'd failed to adequately "leave" his parents in order to sufficiently "cleave" to his wife, in an emotional sense Rod was living the life of a bigamist.

Until this revelation, whenever Rod's dad was depressed, Rod was always there to listen. When his mom was upset with his dad, he was there to listen. If his brother called, usually angry at their dad—you got it—he listened, sometimes for hours on end. Rod would listen and then try to "fix" the problem. His custom was to give his parents and brother advice, then bail them out emotionally so they felt relieved. This was good enough—for a while.

Of course, with this family system pattern in place, no one was ever forced to do anything to improve their relationships. They just used Rod as an emotional dumping ground. Rod had been fulfilling this role since he was a young boy, and the various family members knew their roles well. Theirs was a typical family systems-style arrangement within dysfunctional families. Without intervention, the emotional merry-go-round would have continued to spin. After appeasing the current needy family member demands, Rod "carried" the relative's feelings around with him and became depressed, sometimes for days, sometimes for weeks. He bore within himself the hurt and anger of everyone, like a sponge for all the family pain.

During these periods, Rod was useless as a husband or father. In fact, he'd trained his wife not to bother him during these down times. His depressed state was her signal to withdraw and not share her feelings with him so as not to add to his emotional overload. Then he would gradually come out of his depression and want to be more involved with her.

That's when she got angry. After all, had he not emotionally abandoned her?

The solution was for Rod to emotionally "divorce" his parents so he would not end up divorced from his wife. Perhaps *divorce* is a bit strong of a term, because it doesn't mean that Rod would totally cut off his relationship to his family, but it does mean that the relationship would have to change radically. He could no longer pick up his parents' pain. He had to learn to let them carry their hurt themselves. It was their hurt to carry, not his. Or, in the language of knapsacks and boulders (see chapter 8), it was their knapsack to carry, not his.

It was hard for Rod to learn this lesson because he'd been carrying the family burdens since childhood. As he got honest, he admitted the "fixer role" made him feel important. Abandoning that role would mean losing his special position in the family. In addition, since others would no longer be taking up all his emotional energy, he might have space to look at his own inner life, possibly even share his own struggles and doubts—and that could be frightening. He had been so busy "solving" everyone else's problems, he'd never focused on his own.

After much time and mentoring, Rod was finally able to say in a conversation with his dad, "I don't want to listen to you talk about your problems with Mom. You should talk to her about them. Let's you and I talk about you and me."

Rod's honesty didn't mean he did not love or respect his father. All it meant was that he was refusing to carry his father's knapsack. It was not his burden. With a simple communication, Rod liberated himself from what had become a habitual negative pattern. Moreover, by casting off the burden his father wrongly insisted on placing upon his son, Rod freed up his father to begin recovery himself by forcing him to realize that he needed to deal with his wife, not his son, on such a matter.

What knapsack might you be carrying that might actually be keeping a loved one from the discomfort that could lead to significant change? Remember how clear Jesus was with the "ownership" of the wine shortage problem? He clearly stated that the problem was neither His nor Mary's to solve. Once that was clear, He was free to choose His response to the situation. As noted, apparently Jesus felt that there were spiritual and strategic benefits to honoring the request and meeting the desire. But the greater point was that Jesus knew whose knapsack this was, and that He had complete freedom to say "yes" or "no" to the question at hand.

After Rod got clear on whose knapsack was whose, he could make choices to help out or say "no" without guilt or manipulation, in adult-like freedom.

Carrie struggled with hidden agendas and expectations in a different way. Her parents' marriage was not a close one. Although open conflict was rare, there was a distinct emotional distance between them. Even though

Carrie was a single adult woman with her own career, she could not bring herself to move out of her parents' home and get her own place. She felt a pull to stay and remain "available" for her mother and father. She filled a need in their lives; their world revolved around her.

The payoff cut both ways: Carrie received the warm feeling of being needed in her special role; focusing on their daughter gave purpose to the already dead relationship between Carrie's mother and father. As long as she met that need in them, they would never have to face the emptiness in their marriage.

Yet Carrie, in the prime of her life and quite eligible for dating and marriage, never had a consistent dating relationship. After two or three dates, the men never called her again. One day a close friend commented to Carrie, "I wonder if you are somehow telegraphing to the men you are dating that you are already emotionally committed?" A lightbulb came on as she recognized the truth of that observation. Carrie's bargain within her family system was to stabilize her parents' marriage; in return, their role was to make her feel special. So she did not need a relationship with a young man her age; she "had everything she needed" at home.

When Carrie became aware of this hidden agenda in her family, it frightened her. She was afraid to talk to her parents about it, for fear they would divorce each other. That had been her family "job" after all, to protect them from having to deal with their difficulties. It had somehow been okay for her brothers and sisters to grow up and progress in lives of their own, but for Carrie to do so was unthinkable. Something was obviously awry.

With the support of her siblings (who'd seen the dysfunction all along), Carrie was finally able to talk with her parents about her feelings. In fact, she had two of her wisest siblings join her in a family discussion. At first her parents denied what she was saying; her father basically shamed her for questioning the status quo that was working so well for him and his wife (see chapter 5 for a fuller discussion of shaming). Yet as the conversation progressed and Carrie was able to be firm and direct about her feelings, her mother began to cry uncontrollably.

Her mother admitted she didn't want Carrie to move out. Carrie's arrival home at the end of her workday was the only part of the day her mother could look forward to. Carrie's mother desperately "needed" to have Carrie play her dysfunctional role. The pain of not having Carrie around—and of having to address issues with her husband—was terribly frightening to her mother.

Just as Jesus firmly and honestly addressed His mother at the wedding in Cana, Carrie needed to say strongly, directly, respectfully, and firmly to her parents, "Mom and Dad, I need to move out. Deep down in my heart, I'm afraid to do that because you depend so much on me. I'm afraid your marriage won't survive and that I'm the one who is keeping you together. But it's not right that I should continue to play this role. You two have got to deal with each other, and I've got to get on with becoming emotionally independent."

Carrie saw bringing those feelings out of the closet as a sign that she was somehow being disloyal to or disrespectful of her family. Yet hiding the truth was keeping her from becoming all that God meant for her in adulthood. Slowly and painfully Carrie did reeducate herself on these and other topics by reading some books on codependency (a family system in which unspoken agreements keep everyone stuck in unhealthy communication). It took a lot of courage for Carrie to grow up and take ownership of her own life. Codependence, in her case, meant she had assumed she must take care of her parents and that her own needs did not matter. She had assumed that if she loved her parents fully enough and was good enough to them, they would give her love and approval. Her worth and value as a person rested on their response to her.

When she did move out, her parents' relationship did indeed deteriorate. Their arguments became more frequent and more heated. Her mother had several "crises" that were in reality attempts to pull Carrie back into a caretaking role. But when Carrie gave her mother support from a distance, validating her mother's ability to handle her own problems but refusing to move back in, the message was clear: Carrie was separating in healthy, albeit belated, ways. Eventually Carrie learned not to feel guilty for the turmoil her parents managed to get themselves into, and to let them carry their burdens by themselves.

Amazing, isn't it, when we realize there was potential tension and conflict in Jesus' human family? But we need not be surprised, for in Jesus' human family there was only one divine member. I think we often let some of Jesus' divinity rub off on Mary and Joseph and let that color our reading of passages involving His parents. We know that the perfect Son never even got close to interacting with His parents or other family members in a dysfunctional way, yet there were occasionally less-than-perfect responses to events from among His human loved ones.

There was nothing bad or shameful in what happened at Cana between Jesus and His mother. It was a normal process that needed to occur between Jesus and His family; it was a normal clash between the human (Mary) and the divine (Jesus). The clash showed a growing, healthy independence in which Jesus did not always agree with His mother.

Jesus' healthy response was actually similar to a response He had made to His parents years earlier when He was just twelve, the age of transition from boyhood to manhood.

"LOST" IN THE TEMPLE

As the story unfolds in Luke 2:41–52, Joseph and Mary had made their regular pilgrimage to celebrate the Passover in Jerusalem and were journeying back to Nazareth. They were one day's journey back toward home when they realized their twelve-year-old son was not, as they had supposed, with another family or somewhere else in their traveling party. Panic struck, and they immediately headed back to Jerusalem to search for Him.

Imagine for a minute that you had driven to Los Angeles for some occasion, and that during your return trip to the East Coast, you stopped overnight in New Mexico and realized your son was missing. You thought he was in a friend's car. Your mind begins to race. *Where is that rascal? Didn't he know he was supposed to ride with the Jones family? What's happened to him by now?* Your feelings are a mixture of fear for his safety and anger that he has upset the normal pace of the return trip.

Joseph and Mary spent a day traveling back to Jerusalem, then three more days looking for Him in that huge city. Jesus had been on His own for five days! Those days of wandering about in the Holy City are interesting, for during that entire period, Jesus' parents seem not to have made the link between Jesus' interests and His probable whereabouts.

Jesus observed and commented on that very point when they finally found Him: "Why is it that you were looking for Me? Did you not know that I had to be in My Father's house?" (Luke 2:49). He seems to be saying, in effect, "Why did you wander about Jerusalem for three days? Don't you know me well enough to have guessed I'd be here, discussing the things of God?" Mary and Joseph seem to have had the same difficulty parents today have in understanding our developing teenagers: They responded in knee-jerk fashion. What they needed to do was tune in to their son's motivations and interests, to try to understand the unique person in their midst and not let their own dreams, aspirations, or busy agendas overlook who He was.

When Mary and Joseph find their son, Mary uses a shame-based accusation in her first words with Him. The Living Bible puts Mary's exclamation so well: "Why have you done this to us? Your father and I have been frantic, searching for you everywhere" (2:48).

Again, Jesus does not respond in a codependent way. He doesn't reply, "Oh, I'm sorry, I feel terrible that you have been so worried and hurt. I know that it's my responsibility that you are feeling panicked—your feelings and reactions are really not your responsibility. And it's probably my fault you've not been trusting Jehovah to keep me safe over the last few days. Mom and Dad, would you please forgive me for treating you so badly?"

Rather, Jesus responds directly, clearly, and to the point. There is no guilt or shame in His response. He says that He is about His Father's business and that His Father's house would have been a logical place to look for Him! In a sense, this event is Jesus' declaration of independence at the brink of adulthood, and it is very difficult for His parents to accept.

Was it hard for your parents to understand your interests and accept your growing independence when you were a teen? Or are you having trouble as a parent accepting the increasing autonomy of your teenagers? I'm not saying that parents of teens need to exert zero control over their kids. I'm only saying that the degree of control during adolescence needs to be at an appropriate level. We need to stay considerably out of the way as our teens develop and be careful not to smother them with our lack of understanding and / or dependency needs.

To illustrate, let me share the case of Valerie, a fifteen-year-old Christian girl whose parents brought her in for a counseling session. The problem, explained the parents, was Valerie's "obsession with boys." As we explored the situation, I found that in reality Valerie was not showing an abnormal preoccupation with boys; in fact, she was not even pressuring her parents for permission to date, as many fifteen-year-olds naturally do.

Yet her parents were convinced she was becoming sexually active, and they grilled her when she came home from school or church events. They were constantly imagining her involved in premarital sexual relationships, when in reality they were just innocent friendships. *The parents, as it turned out, were the ones with obsessive issues.*

As we explored family-of-origin issues with Valerie's parents, we discovered that Valerie's father had watched his father treat his mother with constant disdain. His father had consistently cheated on his wife, communicating to his son, Valerie's father, that women were good for one thing only. Valerie's mother grew up in an alcoholic family and had been sexually molested as a child. When Valerie's mother reached dating age, she became sexually active and wound up "having to" marry Valerie's father. Family patterns were coming out into the open, and Valerie's parents' preoccupation with teenage sexual issues began to make sense. They were parenting out of fear. They had not dealt with their own issues, and this was putting a spin on their parenting of a young, healthy, vibrant Christian daughter like Valerie.

From Jesus' courageous example of facing up to shaming parents, we can take heart to face our own family dysfunctions straight on. One such person who learned that it's okay to face crippling problems directly was Jessica.

Jessica grew up as a person whose mission in life was to please and take care of everyone. It was as though she had neon signs on her forehead that blinked, "I'm here to serve and take care of you. I'll serve you. My feelings and needs are unimportant."

When she married Bill she was attracted to his strong Christian commitment and his manly strength. She felt safe with him, which is something she had never felt growing up in her alcoholic family. As time progressed, she discovered her "perfect man" had problems with alcohol and porn. This frightened her, as she didn't know how to react.

Her pastor emphasized that she should simply stay submissive and "love her husband into reform." So Jessica doubled up her efforts to be "perfect" and went into Christian service hyperdrive. If someone needed a thousand cookies for some church event, she would bake them. If someone needed her to "fill in" in the church nursery for twelve weeks in a row, she would do it.

As her husband's alcoholism and sexual addiction progressed, his sexual demands on her became more intense. She became a sex object to him, which grieved her. In time, she became cold toward him, though she felt great internal shame about it. It meant to her that she was not being a good, submissive, Christian wife. She couldn't see that her cold feelings were a normal response to an incredibly insane situation.

Jessica's recovery began when she attended her first Al-Anon meeting. (Al-Anon is a recovery group for relatives of alcoholics that has decades of experience in helping those who live with addicted loved ones learn to respond in ways most healthy for all in the family.) One of the most difficult steps for Jessica was to tell her Christian friends that she was finding help in Al-Anon. Most of them, in lockstep with the pastor's distortion of Scriptures about submission, had encouraged her not to go. But it was in that Al-Anon group that Jessica learned how to stop covering up for her husband's addictions and let him begin to face the consequences of his actions. She learned how to "respond to" and not "react to" the insanity of his alcoholic cycles.

These difficult steps of recovery were her first movements toward making her home emotionally safe for herself and her children. As strength began to build in her she was able to say to her husband, with the help of a trained interventionist, "Bill, either you go into treatment now for your addictions, or you leave this house." A strong statement, true, but her husband, who had been abusing Jessica and her kids, did enter treatment that very day. Jessica's direct approach to addressing problems ushered in an era of recovery for her family.

FAMILY SYSTEMS RESIST CHANGE

Another interaction between Jesus and His human family is recorded in Scripture. It is an amazing event, yet it is consistent with the interactions we have examined so far. It had to do with Jesus' relatives' reactions to the public response to His ministry:

> Then Jesus entered a house, and again a crowd gathered, so that he and his disciples were not even able to eat. When his family heard about this, they went to take charge of him, for they said, "He is out of his mind." . . .
>
> Then Jesus' mother and brothers arrived. Standing outside, they sent someone in to call him. A crowd was sitting around him, and they told him, "Your mother and brothers are outside looking for you."
>
> "Who are my mother and my brothers?" he asked. Then he looked at those seated in a circle around him and said, "Here are my mother and my brothers! Whoever does God's will is my brother and sister and mother" (Mark 3:20–21; 31–35 NIV).

This point in his ministry marked a special time in Christ's life. He had just selected His team of key men, and His ministry was starting to take shape and gather momentum. As He took these important steps, He separated Himself further from His family and marked out His chosen course in life. He was following God the Father's special call on His life—but the change was traumatic for His family members.

It was so traumatic, in fact, that verse 21 says they came to collect their kinsman, since He had "obviously" lost His mind! Can you imagine what this situation must have been like for Jesus' parents and siblings? Their brother and son had left Joseph's carpentry shop and struck out on His own. To them, it must have seemed just like Jesus' behavior when He was twelve years old in the Temple incident. *There he goes again*, they must have thought. It must have worried and embarrassed them that He was causing such a public ruckus. They would take things in their own hands and bring Him home.

Often in families it is difficult for parents and siblings to accept a deviation from the family pattern, no matter how healthy the new course might be or how unhealthy the old course was. I remember finishing college and becoming aware that I was going on to graduate school and would not be going home to work with my dad on our family's farm. That was a sad time for my father. His dream was that all his sons would farm with him. Yet the direction God would have me to go was different.

I felt sad as well, since working on the farm with my father was something I enjoyed. It was painful for me to share my personal vision with my father; those few months were a time of unspoken grief and loss. My father and I did not know how to discuss it, yet the sadness developed into something we felt between us. It was a hard but necessary step of change in my life and a challenging transition within our family.

For many, if not most families, any significant transition can have difficult moments. In troubled families the normal stages of growth and independence may feel as if they are posing a threat. When the son chooses a different path from the father's, that choice is often met with guilt and shame. When he brings the attention of the community upon the family, the family system often resists the new course. In the case of Jesus' human kinsmen, it was no different.

Dysfunctional families often believe that they (and only they) know what's best for the non-conforming family member. It's like the middle-aged mother who says curtly to her teenager, "Will you please put on a sweater? I'm cold!" She assesses what's best for the other person out of her own need, not out of informed concern for the other.

Jesus was right in the middle of setting the foundation for His three-year public ministry. It was time for Him to press forward in a special way, but pressing forward did not match up with what the family perceived as being best for Him.

How did Jesus respond? He didn't say, "Yes, Mom, I'm coming. I'll be right there." He didn't turn to everyone around Him and say, "It's time for me to go home. Come back again tomorrow, and maybe Mom will let me talk with you then."

Instead He strongly, directly, and firmly asked the rhetorical question, "Who are my mother and my brothers?" (Mark 3:33 NIV). Then He answered His own question, motioning to those sitting around Him and saying, "Behold, My mother and My brothers! For whoever does the will of God, he is My brother and sister and mother" (vv. 33–35 NASB).

It was a strong statement, first to His family and then to the people around Him. In just a couple of sentences Jesus fully responded to the issues underlying His family's attempt to "take custody" of Him. He did not argue, did not become defensive, did not give in and say, "All right, Mom, whatever you want."

Instead, He clearly, firmly, directly, and respectfully said, in effect, "This is My new life. These people understand who I really am, and if you want to see Me as I really am, then you are My mother, brother, and sister." These are powerful words that came from deep down within our Savior's heart.

The next verse (4:1) describes Jesus teaching by the sea. So many people crowded on the shore that He had to get into a boat and drift out a little way from the shore to teach from the boat.

What if Jesus had chosen to go back to Nazareth, back into His family's care, as they urged Him to do? God the Father had a different plan in mind for Jesus, and He was determined to follow it.

Jesus acted authentically, in honest accord with Who He really is, and took the bold steps necessary to fulfill God's call on His life. We should follow His example, regardless of how shrill are the cries of troubled family members who want to hinder our growth and pull us back into old patterns of behavior and thinking. We can honestly tell them, just like Jesus did, that true family are those who respect and acknowledge God's call on each individual life.

Sometimes that respectful, loving family is related by blood, but I've often seen people create a healthy and functional family from mentors, peers, and wise brothers and sisters in the family of God. Healthy families encourage the freedom to follow God as each individual sees or hears from him. It may not always be easy, but this is the path of growth, wisdom, and healthy relating.

Questions for Reflection

1. What was life like for you as a teenager? Did your family have difficulty with either the direction you took in life or the strengths you showed as you developed?

2. When Jesus was asked by His mother to make the wine, He replied, in effect, "The timing is not right." Were there times when you felt pushed by your family to do something or to behave a certain way before you were inwardly ready?

3. Can you also think of a time when you preferred not to do something, and said so, but decided to honor the request out of a higher reason? What is the difference between obeying your adult parents and honoring them?

4. Mark 3:20–35 records how Jesus' family thought He had lost His senses when He began His ministry. They were concerned that He was not taking care of Himself. When you first began your recovery program or first began to face the issues dominating your family of origin, did your family think you were crazy or try to make you "come home" by returning to the old ways of doing things?

PART TWO

CONTRIBUTING FACTORS IN
FAMILY DYSFUNCTION

4

Passing the Torch:
The Multigenerational
Transmission Process

Dave Carder

THE PAIN of that night back when he was thirteen years old had been overwhelming for Jim. When Dad said he was leaving the family, that he had another girlfriend, and that he wouldn't be back, Jim couldn't believe it. He thought it was some cruel joke. His father's reassurances that he would still provide for them and would still see them on weekends were lost in Jim's unbelieving numbness. When it finally sank in that Dad wasn't kidding, Jim fled upstairs to his bedroom sobbing.

Finally, he heard his dad's car start in the driveway. Going to the window, he saw the car back out and pull away. Tears streaming down his cheeks, Jim watched the taillights until they were out of sight. The memory of that event still made Jim cry, and that was true even tonight, at forty-three, as he drove the U-Haul truck across the Kansas plains.

Back east were his wife and family, in emotional shambles. Following closely behind the truck was his girlfriend, Sally, driving her late-model car. They were headed west for a new life together. He was in his middle forties, she in her late twenties.

He had never intended to do this. In fact, on that night so long ago and many times thereafter, he vowed that for him marriage would be "forever." He would never abandon his kids. Growing up had been tough, but he had made it. He had always managed to keep his grades up, work part-time during school, and still play sports. After a great high school baseball season, he won a college scholarship, then went on for his M.B.A. and marriage.

Jane had been great, and their early marriage had been, well, pretty good. Work was tough, but Fortune 500 corporations demand long hours—besides, he wasn't scared of hard work. But things in their marriage went sour, and something snapped in him. Now he was going to try again with Sally. He knew Jim Jr. was sobbing his heart out back home, just as he had done as a boy.

He hated even to think about that boyhood scene so long ago. Nobody had ever allowed him to talk about it. Mom had said that they just had to go on. The incident was over, she said, and they couldn't change it. Pastor said that he should forgive his dad, and Jim thought he had. He did pray about it once, at least.

Now on this dark night it seemed so unfinished. Jim wondered if this was what his dad had felt like. Before long Jim had to pull to the shoulder of the highway because he was crying so hard. He felt like going back, in a way, but he didn't. He just couldn't. He didn't know why and, what's more, he wasn't sure he even wanted to know the answers to those questions.

When he had recovered somewhat, and after he had muttered some excuse for his behavior to a somewhat puzzled Sally, he and his girlfriend drove on into the lonely Kansas night.

THE "SINS OF THE FATHERS"

The pattern of a father (or a mother, for that matter) passing infidelity on to a child is heartbreaking. But until Jim figures it out, he very likely will pass on to his son what he hated most about his own childhood. The more an individual understands his or her past, the greater the possibility that he or she will be able to control what he or she passes on to the next generation. The term *understanding* here means more than just knowing the facts, though that is where you start, especially since dysfunctional families tend to hide hurtful facts.

LOOKING CLOSELY AT WHAT IS OFTEN "OVERLOOKED"

The following questions are ones you can use to find out more about your past. Most of these questions are painful to think about, but they deal with very influential people in a family tree, so it is important to consider them. Separating fact from fiction is sometimes like detective work, but it is a necessary first step in stopping a pattern of dysfunction. Otherwise, the secrets at the heart of a family's dysfunction will remain hidden in the family's version of events and thus be locked off from useful access. Only much later, after valuable time is lost, will anyone be able to sort it all out.

1. Who is/are the individual(s) in your family tree about whom other family members are the most quiet?

2. Who is most frequently blamed for family problems, i.e., who is the "black sheep" or "the bad kid"?

3. Who was unable to stay married for a very long time or, if presently married, has been unfaithful? Do you see a correlation of events in the present with what happened to that person in his or her childhood?

4. Who is/was the addict in the family tree? What was his (her) pain? How does the family view him (her)?

5. Who was cut off from the family tree? Who stayed away of his or her own volition? Who was ignored at family gatherings?

6. Who (if anyone) in your family suffered from a serious or chronic illness? What purpose did the illness serve? How has the emotional pain it produced been "medicated"?

7. Who in your family manifests the often stress-related illnesses such as allergies, chronic back pain, headaches, or gastrointestinal difficulties?

8. Who in the family was depressed, suicidal, or even hospitalized for mental illness?

9. Who was angry, mean, and/or controlling in your family?

10. Which parent had the most power in your family? How did he/she use it? How did that parent maintain power and keep everybody in line?

These questions can help bring hidden problems to your attention. There's a good reason the issues have stayed hidden, because families tend to follow unwritten rules that enable family secrets to stay secret. When all family members "agree" to keep quiet about such secrets, those secrets become powerful, though unacknowledged, shapers of behavior.

FAMILY RULES GOVERNING FAMILY SECRETS

A specialist in recovery, Claudia Black[1] has identified three almost universal family rules in dysfunctional families. They are: Don't Talk, Don't Trust, and Don't Feel.

- Every family uses *some* of these rules *some* of the time. This point is related to the earlier observation that all families are somewhat dysfunctional.
- Some families use *some* of these rules *all* of the time. Families tend to see the rules they use as self-evident and always desirable, without question.
- Some families use *all* of these rules *some* of the time. That will usually occur in families with recurring stress patterns, for example, families that have experienced frequent job-related transfers, chronic illnesses, and so on.
- Some families use *all* of these rules *all* of the time. These families have in place the most lethal of family patterns. With no outlet for his feelings, a child in such a family never blossoms into full identity. He or she just strives to survive.

Don't Talk

Family thinking under this rule goes something like this: "Don't talk to anyone outside our family about what you see going on in our family. This is normal family life. Everyone will think you are stupid if you see it other-

1. Claudia Black, *It Will Never Happen to Me* (Center City, Minnesota: Hazelden, 2001), 27–46.

wise. Don't talk about it within the family, either, okay? Stay on safe subjects; pretend everything is okay. Who knows; maybe it will become okay if we pretend long enough. Don't ask questions! That is dangerous—you will upset someone. Remember, we are a family. No one else really understands our family, so don't try to explain it to anyone. That would be foolish. Besides, you don't know who can be trusted outside the family."

The question of trustworthiness leads to the second rule.

Don't Trust

"Don't trust anybody outside the family. Who knows what they might do to or say about our family? You don't want to be responsible for that, do you? Besides, their families are just like ours. You need to care for us, not worry about them. Our family depends upon you—don't let us down. However, don't lean on me, as I am leaning on the bottle. So what if I got a little carried away last night? Everybody does that once in a while." You can substitute any number of addictions for that last reference to drinking—for example, workaholism or hyperperfectionism.

Trust is discouraged within the family through broken promises and failed commitments. The failure of parents to follow through with what is important to their children fuels this mistrust. The parents may be notable for their lack of attendance at their children's performances in sports, music, or drama. They may fail chronically to pick up their children on time (or at all) after events, thus keeping them waiting or dependent upon others to find transportation. They may impose an inordinately restrictive dress code on their children as a result of overly restrictive family standards in general or of parental distortions ("body piercing and tattoos are of the devil"). There are many ways a parent's dysfunction can grossly affect children. But whatever path is taken, the lack of trust built up through failed commitments develops hurt, shame, embarrassment, and anger in the child.

The child, unable to talk (the "Don't Talk" rule in operation), now experiences an eroding trust factor and emotional shutdown. She quietly asks herself, *If my parents—who are supposed to care for me—won't nurture me, who will?* She begins to shut down emotionally. It is too scary to risk herself emotionally in such an atmosphere.

Don't Feel

"If you won't allow yourself to think about the situation, it won't hurt so bad. After all, you really don't hurt that badly. Those are just silly, childish emotions. It's better to put them out of your head completely. That way you'll make it through life a lot better. Besides, you just think you have it tough. You ought to have seen what it was like in my family" (or other families in the neighborhood).

Denial begins to reshape the perceptions of the family. Some sense has to be made out of its craziness, so unfinished business goes underground to resurface in the next generation. The child begins to say to himself, *I am not going to get what others have* (for example, love and a normal level of family function), *but then again I guess I don't need it either.* Feelings freeze up. Spontaneity is lost. It doesn't hurt so badly anymore, but a key aspect of the child's nature—his emotional expression—has atrophied. It's a tragedy.

When a child shuts down his painful emotional side, he also loses the ability to express his joyous side. Emotions are a whole. With anger comes the ability to express delight; with sadness comes the ability to express lightheartedness. This is the breadth of emotion that allows an adult to experience intimacy with a spouse, with God, and with his children.

Some families actually use statements that squelch emotions. "If you don't quit crying, I'll give you something to cry about!" "You shouldn't feel that way." "Children should be seen and not heard." Other families discount children's hurts. "You'll get over it." "Be tough—it will happen many times, so get used to it." Other families don't see how insane it is for parents to expect their kids to be little adults. These individuals often report the feeling of having had to grow up too fast. Attitudes like these help form aberrant patterns.

Though feelings are a package given to us by God, they are often influenced by culture. When internal spontaneity goes, the child as an adult will have to look externally to the culture to find out what is appropriate at a particular time in his development. For instance, our culture tells young males that anger is okay, but tears are not. Since young males often express their feelings through their hormones, sex and anger become their dominant emotions. With few feelings registering internally, that kind of man becomes insensitive to his own child's hurts. The process that damaged his life is already starting to reoccur in his child. Unless something is done to reverse the pattern, the next generation will be engulfed in it.

CHILDREN'S STYLES FOR COPING WITH FAMILY SECRETS

Dysfunction is passed down from generation to generation in a six-step process, outlined in table 4.1.

As the child develops in a family that structures its interactions around the rubric "Don't talk, don't trust, don't feel" (step 1), a personal pattern emerges. This pattern becomes a preference that later develops into a coping mechanism. It becomes deeply entrenched in behavior because it represents security, freedom from pain, and control over the environment (step 2).

As the child's coping mechanism becomes defined (step 3), a role emerges, which serves to reassure the child that he belongs (step 4). Regardless of how dysfunctional the role is, the family system becomes self-reinforcing—the more he practices it, the more he feels like he belongs to the family; the role becomes his critical link to the family group. That is why roles are so resistant to change, even if tremendous carnage has resulted. The adage "Don't rock the boat" (often used in troubled families) means in this application, "Don't change your role! There is too much uncertainty and chance for pain if you do, so you must keep acting that way."

When a child grows up in such an environment and enters adolescence with its dating and marriage involvements, he will attempt to build new relationships on the same unhealthy pattern (step 5). Those relationships will work initially only if he is able to replicate the same family pattern he came from (remember, his style was forged within a specific family system). Now, as he faces marriage, with tool in hand (with its expected result of a sense of belonging), he will attempt to build a new family unit around his style (step 6).

But beware if the "match" is not perfect! Major problems occur when the new partner has not had the time to adjust, or having the time, refuses to fit into the role his spouse's family system "tool" requires. It's like trying to drive the proverbial square peg into a round hole. Success is practically impossible.

TABLE 4.1

The Interactional Pattern That Passes Dysfunction from One Generation to the Next

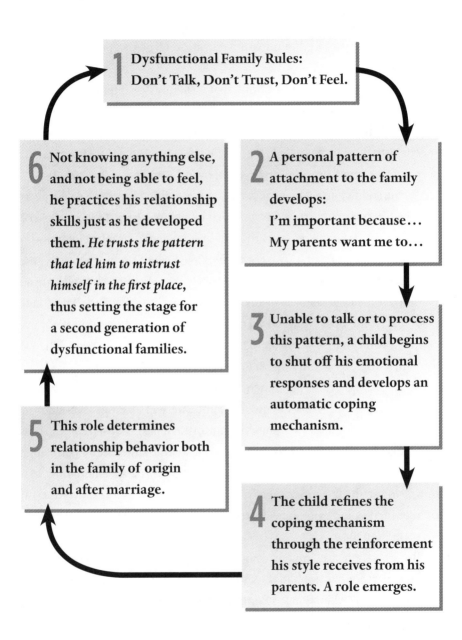

1 Dysfunctional Family Rules: Don't Talk, Don't Trust, Don't Feel.

2 A personal pattern of attachment to the family develops: I'm important because... My parents want me to...

3 Unable to talk or to process this pattern, a child begins to shut off his emotional responses and develops an automatic coping mechanism.

4 The child refines the coping mechanism through the reinforcement his style receives from his parents. A role emerges.

5 This role determines relationship behavior both in the family of origin and after marriage.

6 Not knowing anything else, and not being able to feel, he practices his relationship skills just as he developed them. *He trusts the pattern that led him to mistrust himself in the first place,* thus setting the stage for a second generation of dysfunctional families.

When the individual is not able to replicate his family style and is also unable to develop a new, mutually acceptable pattern with his spouse or child, intense conflict and the destruction of the relationship will occur. That is why these individuals typically go through so many relationships prior to marriage and so many divorces afterward. Witness the woman who marries three alcoholic men in a row, all of whom mercilessly beat her. How could she have "the bad luck" to marry such men? we ask, but the "luck factor" was really very small. Rather, in her marriages, commitment to the relationship has been built on a coping mechanism: "I will stay with you as long as you allow me to live the way I learned to live at home." That is exactly why you hear so many times in troubled marriages, "You drive me crazy! You're *just like* your (expletive deleted) father/mother!"

The most important phrase in the process is found in step 6: *He trusts the pattern that led him to mistrust himself in the first place.* That is why the pattern becomes so important. There is nothing else to fall back on. The individual says to himself, *This is the only style I know. I am afraid to change because I can't trust. I can't feel, so I have no internal validation on which to rely as I go through the process. I can't talk about all that is going on, so I stay angry that the patterns are becoming different.* See the three "Don't" rules at work here?

FAMILY STRUCTURE THAT PROTECTS AND PASSES ALONG FAMILY SECRETS

Family *structure* is different from family *style*. Family style is concerned with how the family comes across to others. It has to do with who appears to be in charge of the family and who *appears* to be responsible for certain items (maybe in accordance with a particular Christian denomination's tradition).

Family structure has to do with the way the family organizes itself around certain individuals. Family structure has to do with who really has power in this family, who really calls the shots. The healthier the family, the less difference there is between style and structure. In a healthy family things are as they appear to be. The greater the differences between style and structure, however, the greater and more powerful the family secrets and dysfunction.

Indeed, family secrets can often take on lives of their own. They become a force within the family simply because so many individuals put so much energy into ignoring, denying, or distorting what has actually happened within the family. As the family tree grows up it incorporates this distortion.

Family structure was initiated in the garden of Eden when the first family composed of Adam, Eve, and God was established. They were close and enjoyed unrestricted intimacy. The fall changed not only that relationship but also the regulations that govern family systems. An understanding of those changes is essential to grasping how and why families develop healthy or unhealthy systems. Let us look at how relationships in the family changed after the fall.

Notice the triangular diagrams in the following pages. They are examples of triad models, diagrams helpful in interpreting relationships in a family. The models operate according to the following assumptions:

1. Often it is helpful to view family relationships in threesomes (triads).
2. Relational intimacy can only be built along one axis at a time. That is why time alone with each family member and time alone with God is important.
3. The relationship between any set of three individuals (a triad) can be evaluated along varying degrees of closeness: *close, cool,* or *conflictual.* All three terms are relative and flex with each family system. *Close* is simply the closest of the relationships, whereas *cool* is slightly more distant or withdrawn than the close relationship, and *conflictual* is more tense, with more open disagreement than in the close relationship.
4. Each triad can only have one *close* relationship, one *cool* relationship, and one *conflictual* relationship at any given time. When a different relationship in a set becomes *close,* the entire pattern changes.
5. The more dysfunctional the family is, the more marked the contrasts between the three relationships.
6. Circumstances can temporarily change the usual pattern of relationships within the triad (for example, the loss of a job, moving to a new city, a major illness, financial reversal, the aging of parents, children moving in / out of the home, and so on).

7. All three relationships are subject to change when one individual in the triad is replaced by another (divorce, death, older parents, children moving in and out of the home, and so on).

TABLE 4.2
Triad Relationship of Adam, Eve, and God

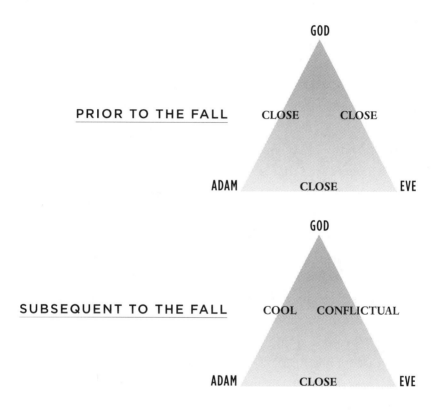

Table 4.2 shows one way the family system in Eden could be diagrammed before and after the fall. Note that the relationships between Adam/God and Eve/God are different. Eve led the rebellion by eating the fruit, so her relationship with God immediately after the disobedience was the rockier one. Adam joined in eating, too, and he must bear responsibility with Eve to be sure, but at least he and God were still on speaking terms, as evident in God's asking Adam, "Where are you?" (Genesis 3:9). Adam and Eve then collaborated in hiding and in clothing their nakedness.

The post-fall triangle only describes the experience just before Adam and Eve left the garden. Relationships are constantly changing, are constantly subject to ebb and flow. Any triad evaluation is only good for the moment. It is simply a snapshot of the relationship. That is true of the triads given above. Eve's relationship with God warmed after she left the garden, as is shown in Genesis 4:1, 25, when she gives credit and thanks to God. A triad evaluation made then might look quite different from the one given in table 4.2.

The relationship between any two persons at the bottom of the triangle will vary depending on the identity of the party at the top (by the way, placement at the top doesn't necessarily imply elevated status). Think about how your family shifts when the two different mothers-in-law come to visit.

Triad relationships have a built-in tension, as you can see. As a counteractive to this confusion, boundaries need to be constructed between the various members of the triad (for a fuller examination of boundaries, see chapter 8). God Himself recognized the trauma of trying to bring parental relationships into the triad relationship of man and wife and gave an explicit command to newly marrieds: for family health, the couple must separate from their respective families of origin and "cleave" to one another (Genesis 2:24; see also chapter 10 of this book).

The triad system of examining relationships is dynamic and flexible. That is because relationships themselves are dynamic and subject to change. When one relationship in a triad changes, the entire system changes to accommodate it.

Now a question is probably surfacing: If relationships operate in triads, how would you diagram an entire family system at once? Table 4.3 provides an answer. Look at all of those triangles! And each axis of each triad has one of three different characteristics. No wonder successful family living is so complicated!

As you study table 4.3, try labeling each axis from your point of view as it pertains to your present family or your family of origin. Then have your spouse make his/her assessment independently of yours, and compare notes. Or ask your adolescent children to label as many triangles as they can. It will make for interesting conversation!

TABLE 4.3

Triad Relationships in a Family

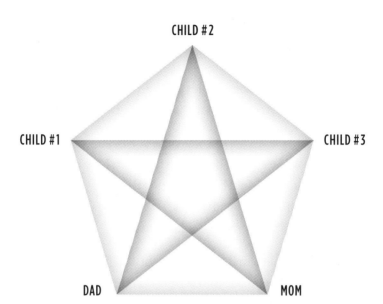

The exercise can lead to significant discoveries and, ultimately, toward the healing of troubled relationships.

PASSING THE TORCH UNCONSCIOUSLY

In summarizing the process that passes dysfunction from one generation to another, we see several elements. We see family rules (don't talk, don't trust, don't feel), and structures (triads). We also see families deciding to disregard God's guidelines for healthy family living (for example, an individual not "leaving" father and mother to "cleave" to a spouse). These patterns result in the "sins of the fathers" being passed down the family tree with alarming predictability.

Let me close this chapter by calling attention to an entertaining observation that also carries with it a sobering truth. It can take a new couple many years, even a lifetime, to sort out which patterns from their respective families of origin they want to keep and which they want to throw away. The influence of their families extends to every sphere of the marital relationship. Which is why I say that when you hop into bed on your wedding night, you will find six people in there: *her* mom and dad, *your* mom and dad, and the two of you!

Questions for Reflection

1. Which of the three "don't" rules did your family employ most? What recurring circumstance caused all the rules to be employed at once in your family?

2. As you review the cyclical pattern in table 4.1, how do you feel about the statement "The child begins to trust the system that caused him to mistrust himself in the first place"? What impact has this phenomenon had on your current adult patterns?

3. If this chapter seems to fit your family of origin, what specific relationship styles do you see your siblings carrying into their dating/marital relationships? How about your own relationship styles?

4. The section on triads says that it is possible to develop intimacy with only one person at a time. How do you feel about that? What regular shifts do you see in your key relationships? What one individual seems to have the most influence in your relationships? Why? Is it appropriate for that individual to have that much influence? If not, what options do you have?

5. On a scale of 1 to 10 (with 10 being high), how close was your family's style (the way it looked from the outside) to its structure (the way it actually functioned)? Did the individual who was supposed to be responsible for certain behavior actually carry out that responsibility? If he didn't, who "covered" for him? How would your other siblings answer?

5

Guilt-ridden Baggage:
The Role of Religious Shame

Earl Henslin

GRAB A pencil and check yes or no to the following questions; you'll total the results below. Be honest—this is only a private assessment of your feelings and has proved helpful to many people who have taken it.

Shame Quiz

Do you have difficulty feeling relief when you confess your sin to God or to another person? In other words, do you have lingering feelings of guilt that you've never been quite able to shed?

Yes   No

When other people are having fun, do you feel uncomfortable?

Yes   No

When you feel hurt or angry, do you automatically experience guilt for feeling that way?

Yes   No

Is it hard for you to tell another person how you are feeling because you think he might think you are a bad Christian/person?

Yes   No

Do you feel embarrassed when you experience success?

Yes   No

Is it hard for you to totally relax / have fun?

Yes   No

Do you want to withdraw from friends and family when you feel hurt or when you have done something wrong?

Yes   No

Do you view God as a stern and unfeeling judge you will never be able to please?

Yes   No

Do you feel uncomfortable with and/or have difficulty enjoying your sexuality?

Yes   No

Do you always feel like you will never be a "good enough Christian"?

Yes   No

Are you too quick to criticize and/or judge others?

Yes   No

Do you become defensive quickly whenever someone asks you a question and/or tries to offer constructive feedback?

Yes   No

Are you now depressed and/or angry after reading this list?

Yes   No

Total up your yes answers. Here's an analysis of how you may stand with regard to religious shame:

0–2 *yes* answers: You've been extremely fortunate in not encountering religious shame. You should read this chapter to better understand your spouse, your friends, and your colleagues, who probably have been shamed significantly—or take the week off and go to Hawaii. You deserve it—and you won't feel guilty about it—so go for it!

3–5 *yes* answers: You probably have significant levels of religious shame in your thinking and emotions. You should read this chapter carefully.

6–13 *yes* answers: You'd better find a support group right away!

A SERIOUS MATTER

Even though you may have detected a bit of good-natured humor in this quiz, shame is a serious problem for many, and religious shame even more so, since the power of the Bible or God is purported to back up the person doing the shaming. In other words, nonreligious parents may simply invoke their rank as parents (or invoke cultural traditions) as their authority in making a child feel false guilt. But when religious parents use (or misuse) the Bible as their authority, the effect is far more powerful, long lasting, and resistant to correction. For not only is Mom or Dad shaming the child, but God Himself seems to be in on it, too!

People raised in fundamental religious backgrounds or from shame-based cultures often have to "detox" their thoughts. Religious shaming is not something churches tend to do intentionally or maliciously. Rather, religious shaming reflects a skewed theology, one that leaves out concern for feelings and the inner, emotional life. Emotions are seen as an enemy that needs to be fought, subdued, and controlled by developing a rigid system of good and bad, right and wrong.

Those who have been subjected to this philosophy have had to live with contradictory religious messages, such as:

"I'm as worthless as rags." vs. *"I'm of immense value as a person because Christ died for me."*

"I'm deserving of hell." vs. *"I'm made in God's image."*

It is easy to see why there is widespread confusion and why religious shame is so powerful. Many Christians have been so obsessed with the reality of their "sin nature" that they never allow themselves to enjoy God's grace and the gifts He's given them to enjoy, even celebrate. They have a fear-based outlook and are terrified that if they ease up on over-focus on the continuing struggles with sin, the church will turn into a raging herd of hedonists!

I think it would be great if we could all say at the beginning of a Sunday school class, as in an AA meeting, "Hi, my name is Earl, and I am a sinner." Then everyone would respond in unison with an affirming, "Hi, Earl." That way we'd have that particular theological fact covered and could get on to our main tasks: sharing what God is doing in our lives, sharing our pain and our struggles, and exploring ways to better glorify God in our lives. Though the church today often recognizes the pitfalls of shame-based vs. grace-based religion, Christians still have subtle ways of projecting superior "godliness" in a variety of ways.

Religious shame keeps many Christians from getting help for their problems and keeps them isolated from others, bearing terrible hurts and secrets in a self-imposed solitary confinement. When they do come in my office for help, most often I cannot help them with their presenting problems before we pause to deal with their religious shame and baggage. I typically have a lot of work to do in helping them lop off skewed and dysfunctional religious teachings before new life can begin to grow.

RELIGIOUS SHAME VERSUS TRUE GUILT

True guilt is that voice we hear inside—and it could be either the Holy Spirit prompting us or prompting our consciences—letting us know that we have done something wrong. When we hear that prompting we need to take steps to deal with the offense we have committed. The process is stated clearly in 1 John 1:9. All we need to do is to acknowledge, or confess, our sin (literally: "errors" or exercises in "missing the mark") to God and repent (do a 180 and head back in the right direction) and we are cleansed from it all—because Christ has already paid our debt.

However, many do not feel forgiven even after they have agreed with God that they've messed up and asked to be cleansed. (See Matthew 18:21–35, where the forgiven servant didn't feel forgiven). The culprit at this point is usually shame, or false guilt. What's the difference between shame/false guilt and true guilt?

Guilt says, *"I've done something wrong."*
Shame says, *"There is something wrong with me."*

Guilt says, *"I made a mistake."*
Shame says, *"I am a mistake."*

Guilt says, *"What I did was not good."*
Shame says, *"Who I am is not good."*

Here's an example of shaming from everyday life. A four-year-old's room is generally messy, right? Now a religious, shame-based parent would scold the child and say, "God thinks that Jamie is a bad and lazy girl since she didn't pick up her toys!" (Such a statement is usually accompanied by the parent's fierce-looking frown.) You can imagine the view of God this practice gives a young, impressionable child! The parent resorted to shaming a child for an age-appropriate behavior, over an issue that should have been lovingly and patiently taught and corrected, not condemned and browbeaten. As this child receives thousands of shame-based messages throughout her development, it will become difficult, as an adult, for her to differentiate between normal guilt (where the goal is forgiveness and loving redirection) and shame (where we beat ourselves up for being unlovable or broken, somehow, at the core of our being).

Those brought up in shaming environments (be they religious or cultural) find it almost impossible to experience true relief and closeness to God after confession of sin, try as they may.

TWO TYPES OF RELIGIOUS SHAME

There are two types of religious shame: *external* and *internal*. External religious shame is experienced from outside of ourselves, when a person, group, or organization inflicts shaming upon us. Internal religious shame is a process that goes on within us, and has to do with messages and feelings we tell ourselves, dictating our reactions to life and others.

External Religious Shame

External religious shame occurs in many forms: a comment or look of superiority, a set of "should or should not" rules for daily living. It is an "ought to" based life.

Religious shame can even subconsciously influence the type of church we choose. We are likely to choose a church that reflects the level of religious shame within us. If we feel more comfortable with an external, rule-governed spirituality that dictates how we are to live, then we will choose that type of church.

Legalistic churches, which are highly controlling of their members, feel safer and more comfortable to the person dominated by religious shame. Life feels easier if the choices of where to go and what to do are pre-made. In a religious organization characterized by shame-based thinking, people don't have to take much personal responsibility for deciding their own conduct under God. They just follow the prescriptive code and feel that they are safely "in" with God.

External religious shame fosters and encourages secrets.

Though there is talk of grace in many churches, some Christians tend to squirm when people really try to be honest about their struggles. How many of us belong to a group of Christian friends where we feel safe talking about real life struggles? Would you be comfortable talking about being tempted by an emotional affair? Struggles with internet porn? Anorexia or bulimia? How about a daughter who is promiscuous? A son who is on drugs? What if you've begun doubting your faith or wondering where God is in your pain? What if your adult child is living with someone instead of getting married, or has a gay partner?

If you are afraid that if you are honest about these common realities, you might be a) talked down to, lectured, or preached to, b) gossiped about (via sharing "prayer requests"), or c) misunderstood and held at arm's length; you may be in a shame-based church or surrounded by shame-based religious family or friends.

When conversations between Christians are limited to a form of spiritualizing that communicates only what is going well and nothing about each others' real life struggles or challenges, people become experts at hiding and covering up their pain.

Comedian Jeff Foxworthy had a popular stand-up routine, *"You Might Be a Redneck If . . ."* Well, "You Might Be in a Shame-Based Environment If . . ." those around you:

1. Are driven by guilt, fear, or overwhelming desire to please.
2. Have a hard time respecting themselves and others in an equal balance.
3. Tend to be aggressive, judgmental, controlling, or mean.
4. Often project their inner anger and other strong emotions onto others.
5. Want others to provide a constant stream of adoration so they can continue to feel good (or superior) to others. (Needing a "narcissistic fix," they fish for compliments to feed their emptiness or cover their inner shame-based self-condemnation.)
6. Are motivated by fear, showing lots of "hyper-vigilant" behaviors. Tend to be super-alert for anything or anyone who might upset the little kingdoms they've mentally created.
7. Resort to black-and-white thinking: Unable to see shades of grey, they prefer to see the world through "my way or the highway" glasses.
8. Appear critical and judging of others. (It may help to know that their inner voice is just as merciless and judging of themselves; they just rarely let on what's really happening within.)
9. Create a façade and like to stay in conversational control. They often take charge and do most of the talking, with little sincere inquiry or deep listening. Their desire is to impress more than to deepen intimacy.

Internal Religious Shame

Internal religious shame is the inner voice that communicates what a failure you are. It is an inner set of beliefs, values, and experiences based on distorted messages or experiences in life. These beliefs usually originate in churches or cultures that are shame-based in orientation. In California, where we have so many people coming from foreign countries, we are doing more and more counseling to help them recover from shame-based elements in their particular cultural systems. We help folks find a balance between honoring their parents and making their own choices for their lives. Otherwise, many adults wake up one day and realize, *I've been living someone else's life!*

When someone has been raised in shame or perhaps was in a marriage where shame was used to belittle and dominate—seemingly insignificant events can trigger a "shame attack" that spirals into depression or anger. For example, Julie's newlywed husband once said, kindly but nonchalantly, "Honey, I'm not crazy about this casserole." Julie immediately went into meltdown mode and began to sob. Paul was amazed at her over-reaction, but as she calmed down, Julie shared that her mother had lived in fear of displeasing her dad at dinnertime. A raging alcoholic, her dad belittled and berated her mom if he didn't like the meal. Julie's stomach still ached when she thought of many dinners ruined by his disappointment and resulting anger. A few times he even threw his plate on the floor and stormed off as the family sat in fearful, shamed silence.

As Paul realized he'd accidentally triggered a painful memory, resulting in his wife's over-the-top response, he held Julie and reassured her that his love, affection, and pleasure in her would never be altered by a less-than-stellar meal. In time she believed him and relaxed. Julie even began to value his honesty about his likes and dislikes because he never talked down to her and he loved to know what she really thought and felt about life's everyday choices. Freedom!

CHARACTERISTICS OF RELIGIOUS SHAME

Shame-based people and religious organizations have a way of looking at life that is radically different from those with a more healthy spirituality. Here are a few examples.

Religious shame says, *"Emotions are bad."*
Healthy spirituality says, *"Emotions are neither good nor bad. It is what you do with them that is important."*

Shame-based religion says, *"Having problems is sinful."*

Healthy spirituality says, *"Having problems is a part of my human condition. I can take my struggles to God and my fellow Christians for support and encouragement."*

Shame-based religion says, *"Compulsive disease is sin."*
Healthy spirituality says, *"Compulsions such as alcoholism, drug addiction, eating disorders, or sexual addiction are complex disease processes that affect a person spiritually, emotionally, and physically. I need to tend to all levels for recovery to occur."*

Let's look a little deeper into some of these shame-based messages.

"Emotions Are Sinful."

Many Christians feel immediately guilty when they experience feelings of anger or hurt. They were taught that the emotion itself is sin, rather than seeing emotions as red flags that signal us to ask some important questions about what's happening both within and without. If you grew up in a family in which the message was clear that it was not okay to feel certain emotions, you experienced some dysfunction. (To a degree almost everyone has some dysfunction in their upbringing because we were raised by humans and not saints.)

If your parents claimed the authority of God to communicate such family rules as "Don't feel this" or "Don't have that emotion," then you were hit with a double whammy. It is sad, but so often true, that people raised in religious homes have to go through more therapy to get to a place of authentic joy and freedom than non-Christians—because they not only have the "parent stuff" to deal with, they were also given a big side order of "religious baggage." Basically they have to sort through all the messages they were given by their parents, sort of like pulling out strands of yarn from a basket and separating the strands into two categories: messages that were biblical and true and messages that were untrue (and often destructive) but wrapped up in the false package of "biblical teaching."

Many Christians were severely traumatized as they grew up. Even though their parents were Christians, destructive problems like alcoholism, sexual addiction, sexual abuse, and physical or emotional abuse were present in their homes. The mixed messages can do a real number on a child's heart that never quite goes away, even in adult life, without loving intervention and help.

One woman, whom I'll call Judy, struggled with depression and suicidal thoughts from the time she was a teenager. In our first counseling session she told me that although she grew up in a "Christian home," her father was an alcoholic. Even that one piece of information was extremely difficult for her to share because it felt shameful to talk about her dad's faults outside the family circle. Her parents had used fear tactics to make sure she kept the family "code of silence"—which, of course, allowed her dad the freedom to do whatever he wanted. She eventually confessed the tragic truth that he'd also sexually abused her. First came waves of grief accompanied by much weeping, then anger, and then acceptance of what happened, and finally forgiving him. This process took *years.*

It was a long road to help Judy recognize the triple whammy she'd received of family shaming, religious shaming, and abuse. During her long period of counseling, it was hard for her Christian friends to accept the intensity of her emotions. When someone in Christian circles is hurting, it brings out the codependent "rescuers" in the crowd. They want to rush in and immediately fix the pain. Judy's well-meaning friends insisted she needed to let go of her anger and forgive her father immediately. In one sense, her friends were right: Forgiveness is the ultimate goal. But when a person is first becoming aware of the enormity of a suppressed violation, he or she needs time to deal with those feelings.

Whenever Judy tried to let go of the pain prematurely, as her friends suggested, she became depressed and suicidal. This only made her feel more defective as a Christian. Her friends' misguided attempts to "hurry up the healing" only shamed Judy more, set back her progress, and prolonged the agony.

Think of it like this. Say you've had major heart surgery and within minutes of coming awake in the recovery room, a group of friends arrive to say, "Okay, now you've had surgery. If you are really a strong and healthy person, you should be able to jump off that table and come out-

side and play a game of basketball with us." We realize instantly how ridiculous and unfair that is, right? But when someone has just been hit with
a trauma or uncovered one in counseling, we want them to heal instantly.

Forgiveness *is* key—but only in due time and only after the individual
has passed through the appropriate steps. Eventually Judy was able to accept that it was all right for her to feel the anger and hurt she had carried
around inside for so long. For the first time she could see in Scripture that
Jesus was a man of great emotion. She could identify with the rage Jesus
felt when He saw the temple being used wrongly. His response was one
of righteous anger, and He threw the moneychangers out. He expressed
His outrage clearly and directly to the ones who were desecrating God's
temple. As she connected that scriptural reality with her own experience,
imagining Jesus as outraged at the crime against her little precious body,
"a temple of God"—the religious shame lifted. She could begin recovery
in earnest.

"Having Problems Is Sinful."

Somewhere along the line we have lost a sense of humanness in the Christian community. An image of perfection has become the goal of spirituality rather than an attitude of acceptance of ourselves and others and an
understanding that we are all imperfect. We have lost the sense that all of
us need a Savior—and need each other, too.

Who has not struggled with depression? Who has not had times when
he wondered if he wanted to be married to his mate during a particularly
rough season? Who has not wanted to ship his teenagers off to some un-
known place until they were ready to support themselves? Who has not
wanted to run away and hide when life became overwhelming? Who has
not struggled with her own "secrets," certain that if people really knew
her they would not want to be around her?

It is normal to have struggles, to have hurts to get over. There is no
such thing as a perfect marriage or a perfect family. Our parents were imperfect, and we are as well. We live in a world much different from the
one in which our parents grew up. We have a much greater opportunity
than they did to deal honestly with feelings, intimacy, closeness, and self-

esteem. The tragedy is that so many—too many—still continue to struggle alone, rather than letting Christ become real to us through the actions of a caring, supportive community.

Please don't misunderstand me on this. God is the cornerstone of any healing process. No lasting change or healing occurs without the Lord. Yet as Rich Buhler, a popular radio pastor in California, used to say, "If you were a lousy cook before you became a Christian, more than likely you will be a lousy cook after you become a Christian." If you did not have the skills to express your feelings, to be close, to be intimate, or to resolve conflicts before you became a Christian, more than likely you will have trouble in those areas after you become a Christian, too.

The difference, though, is that as a Christian you will have the power of the Holy Spirit in your life. He can empower you and motivate you to learn and make the changes needed in relationships. There's a deep sense that Someone is listening on the other end of the line when you pray, and that in and of itself is so healing to our minds and bodies. Especially when you realize how much that Someone loves and cares for you and has compassion for your heartache.

Having problems just means you have an opportunity see God working within your life, often through others who are vessels of His love. As my friend Dave Carder often says, "If you *always* do what you have *always* done, you will *always* get what you have *always* got." Making a change might mean taking the risk of going to a support group or seeking a more spiritually healthy church, where honest sharing takes place. It might mean taking the risk of talking with a recovery-literate pastor or similarly qualified Christian therapist. It does not mean staying alone and isolated with your hurt.

"Compulsive Disease Is Sinful."[1]
This particular attitude has probably killed more people in the Christian community than any other. By restricting our view of compulsive disease to the purely spiritual realm, or by not paying enough attention to the addictive physiological aspects of compulsive disease, we shame Christians who struggle with these addictions and prolong their agony.

Most of us either know or have read about individuals like these:

- The person who struggles with alcoholism and who feels defective as a Christian. He walks the aisle, gives his life to Christ, and within twenty-four hours is using alcohol again.
- The Christian who struggles with anorexia or bulimia, recommitting herself to Christ over and over again, only to begin compulsively eating again once she is alone.
- The Christian man who vows before God never to view porn again and finds himself compulsively searching his computer for porn sites in the wee hours of the morning . . . again.
- The woman who is unable to face her prescription drug addiction, getting two prescriptions filled from two different doctors for the same medication.
- The man who has to have a cigarette every time he steps out of the house. He is more nervous and disagreeable with his family on weekends because he is accustomed to smoking whenever he wants to at work.
- The man who compulsively works sixty to seventy hours a week and manages to fit in several meetings at church besides. He is addicted to the rush of adrenaline he gets from compulsively working and from having a high profile at church. His family hardly knows him anymore while he puts all his energy into polishing his image outside the home and neglects those who love him the most.
- The teen who cannot stop obsessively washing her hands, or checking the locks, or counting the cracks in the sidewalk, or pulling out hair or eyelashes.

1. Let me explain my use of the term *disease*. Many Christians get uneasy at the use of the word to apply to such compulsions as alcoholism or drug abuse. They think, incorrectly, that using the term implies the idea of dismissing personal responsibility for addictive behavior. Alcoholics could then say, in effect, that their behavior wasn't their responsibility any more than their exhibiting flu symptoms would be. But that's not what I mean. By using the term *compulsive disease*, I am saying that the cluster of behaviors, symptoms, and transmission patterns characteristic of the syndrome parallels the patterns characteristic of such conventional diseases as smallpox or even cancer. Compulsive disease is a complex set of biological, emotional, and spiritual variables that can destroy a person's life and the lives of those around him if left untreated. Those who work in the recovery movement have found the disease paradigm a helpful construct in dealing with life-threatening patterns of behavior.

- The woman who goes from lows of depression then swings to major euphoric highs and in that manic state charges up the credit card, acts out in sexually inappropriate ways, and then wakes up to what she's done, overcome with guilt, and goes even further into depression.

Such people struggle within a predictable cycle of "using," then attempt reform, then fail in some way, then return to "using." Unless intervention takes place, the cycle will continue indefinitely. The addict returns to his "drug of choice" (whether it be food, alcohol, TV, sex, gambling, work, or shopping) because the severity of the withdrawal sets him or her up for the next hit. His entire day is wrapped around the moment he can "use" again. His attachment in life is not to God or to people but to his drug of choice.

This is why 12-step groups are so crucial. We need to be around other people struggling with the same disorder in order to learn how to be sober one day at a time. We need to be around others who are struggling honestly and who know all the games, rationalizations, and tricks we perpetrate on ourselves and others in order to stay in the disease cycle. Self-deception cannot continue among others who know the games you play all too well, since they've been there and done the same.

Though 12-step groups have now popped up in many churches, I remember a time when many Christians frowned upon participation in 12-step programs such as Alcoholics Anonymous (AA), charging that foul language was sometimes used in the meetings, that people sometimes smoked when they were there, and that the phrase "Higher Power as we understand Him" was used as a reference to God. That negative attitude kept many Christians in bondage to compulsive disease and kept multitudes of families in pain. I helped pioneer a 12-step program called Celebrate Recovery that meets in many churches, but I've also seen beautiful recoveries from many clients who participated in Alcoholics or Narcotics or Overeaters Anonymous. Sometimes Christians need to humble themselves and accept that we've much to learn from those who may not share our faith, but who have found some keys to sobriety that have unfortunately escaped many churches and religions.

I should also mention that good medications for depression, obsessive tendencies, bipolar disorder, and even alcoholism are often a huge help in recovery. I've seen lives altered and even saved because of changes in diet, supplements, sleep, and exercise together with well-matched medications. That said, 12-step support groups are still the key in maintaining balance or sobriety and, especially, to overcome the culture of shame. One of the ways they help do this is by example. As each person owns his "stuff" and works through forgiving himself, processing healthy guilt, making amends, and trusting God one day at a time to help him through recovery, shame begins to fall away almost as a by-product.

CLIMBING OUT OF THE PIT OF SHAME

Recovery is a process, not an event. In honest recovery there are no quick fixes or cures. Recovery requires openness and honesty before God and a group of people you can trust. Recovery does not occur in isolation. It occurs in relationship with God and other people.

The following list may get you started on the road to recovery and healing from shame.

1. *Write down a list of shame-based attitudes, beliefs, and experiences, and contrast them with the truth as you recognize it.* Writing is one of the important tools of recovery. When you write something down it becomes more tangible and manageable.

2. *Find a support group, preferably one based on the 12-step model, in which you can share your feelings of religious shame.* Here's the most important message of this book so far: For recovery, you need other people in your life. There are many types of support groups. Attend the one appropriate for you and, in time, take the risk and begin to share what hurts. The easiest way to find one is to Google search the kind of support group you seek, to turn up a website with locations and contact people. If you cannot find the sort of support group you'd like, consider starting one!

3. *Learn to respond and not react to external religious shame.* It is not uncommon for a person to feel angry or hurt as he begins to deal with religious shame. So it's important that you direct the anger you feel where it belongs. Don't use that anger as an excuse to pull away from God or the church (unless you realize that you may be in a controlling, toxic church setting). In most instances, religious shame comes unintentionally from people and churches continuing in lockstep with what they have been taught from their parents and religious authorities.

As you become aware of religious shame, you may need to graciously confront people who have shamed you. There is a risk in doing this: Your relationship with that person or church may change. That does not mean that you need to give up the process, but you do need some support if you decide to confront. Check in with a therapist or wise trusted friend to help keep yourself grounded. Eventually you may need to find a church that is more recovery-oriented and accepting of people who hurt. Sometimes people stay in the same church and attend a support group in another community or church. As you grow in your recovery, you may find other people in your congregation who are in recovery. All it takes is two or three people to start a support group.

4. *Determine if your family is the source of shame.* Healing the entire family system of shame would be, of course, ideal. Besides going to family therapy, which may be the ideal start but perhaps unrealistic for many, you can begin to heal the family system simply by making healthy changes yourself. When one person changes, there tends to be a ripple effect. Others in your family may notice and ask you about your newfound freedom and authenticity; they may even be ready to share, listen, and connect. So maybe you can't heal the whole family system, but you can start with deepening relationships with those in the family who are healthier and more open. Start with one small leaf or branch of the family tree.

If your family system or culture is truly toxic, then remember you can create your own "family" of friends who are healthy, supportive, and compassionate. You may need to minimize time with family members who are especially shaming while you are in recovery. Rarely is it necessary to cut off family members completely, and that is a last resort; usually minimizing time and capitalizing on distance are enough to give you the space needed for recovery. But there are instances where you cannot keep both your sanity and a terribly dysfunctional family relationship.

5. *Read the scriptural account of Jesus and the woman at the well.* John 4:5–26 is one of the most important and powerful Scriptures with regard to shame. Simply by talking to a woman, Jesus was breaking the rules. In this period of history, Jews steered clear of Samaritans, so the fact that she was from Samaria meant Jesus was breaking still more rules. Jesus tells the woman to call her husband. He shows His supernatural nature in knowing her extensive history of failed marriages. As they talk, the woman asks Jesus for the water that will never leave her thirsty again. He goes on to tell her more, and by the end of the passage she apparently accepts the living water.

Now for the interesting part with regard to shame: Do you see Jesus judging the woman at the well? Does He condemn her? Not at all! She simply acknowledges that she does not have a husband. She is truthful, and He accepts that and goes on because He is more concerned about her current inner spiritual condition than her history. He does not focus exclusively on what her inappropriate behavior has been. He goes right to her true need: to find the living water, that is God's grace and ability to live life in a higher spiritual realm.

What a contrast to the way we view life! What is your first reaction when you find out someone is in his second or third or fourth marriage? What would be your reaction to a member of your congregation who had already had five husbands and was now living with another man? What would be your reaction if you found out a member of your church was an alcoholic or a sex addict? It is fascinating that in Jesus' conversation with the woman at the well, all it took was for her to honestly acknowledge the truth about her life and Christ moved on to deal with the most crucial need.

Reread the story of the woman at the well, substituting your own name whenever you see the words *Samaritan woman*. When the passage talks about her issues (which are marriage-related) substitute your own issues. Let it sink in that Jesus understands your situation and wants to bring you out of shame and into healing. This exercise can help move this from an intellectual understanding to something you can feel within.

Imagine being at the well with Jesus. You look into His eyes and can feel the love and compassion He has for you.

Questions for Reflection

1. When was the first time, as a child, that you remember feeling ashamed? What "childhood vow" might you have made to yourself so that you'd never have to have that feeling of shame again?

2. Notice when you feel closed and protective inside when you are around certain people. Do you feel as if you are verbally walking on eggshells? These could be people with shame-based outlooks. Now notice the people who make you open up and blossom, relax and want to be real. More than likely these folks have learned a healthy way of relating to others.

3. How have your experiences with shame-based religious people (if you had them) affected your relationship with God today?

6

Blest Be the Tie That Binds: Local Church Family Patterns

Dave Carder

ONE DOES not have to attend very many churches to realize that each has its own distinctive personality. By personality I mean the pattern the church uses to express itself to those outside, the way it conducts its business within, and the hierarchy of values it establishes for those who belong.

We can tell fairly quickly whether or not we will fit in with a particular group of believers. And that is important, for the better the fit and the more numerous the points of contact, the greater the level of comfort and commitment we will feel. So the church has a vested interest in our commitment, just as we have a vested interest in our comfort. But what exactly are the "points of comfort" or "fit" that get the ball rolling in the first place?

THE SEARCH FOR A CHURCH FAMILY "FIT"

Just as people look for spouses who will allow them to practice the relational styles they learned in their dysfunctional childhoods (see chapter 4), so, too, do they look for churches built on relationship styles with which they are familiar. The way the members of a person's family related to each other and to the power base of the family will determine the type of church family that will attract him. It is all he knows of relationships. People who grew up in homes headed by extremely powerful fathers who were accountable to no one are likely to gravitate eventually to churches where the senior pastor operates the same way. I say eventually, because often new converts stay in the type of environment where they first trusted Christ.

UNFINISHED BUSINESS

Many times unfinished business from a family of origin will be acted out within the church family. An individual who left home angry at his father may well find a church home much like his family home and act out lingering resentment toward his father by aggravating the pastor: continually disagreeing with him, being belligerent, spreading damaging rumors. He will not confront his own father, but he is more than happy to confront the bewildered surrogate, his pastor.[1]

The comfort level the new believer seeks from his new church family can become the source of his greatest disappointment. Having chosen a church family relationship style much like the one he knew at home, he fails to realize that each style has its own craziness. It will not be long before a sense of déjà vu permeates his thinking. What he had hoped to leave behind, he now experiences on an even larger scale in the church. Business meetings become replicas of old family feuds, deacons' meetings replace the family council, and the sermons parallel his parents' lectures.

This dread of getting caught in the same family system one experienced as a child drives some people from church to church, forever looking for the right kind of church family experience. These people are running around issues, not working through them. Individuals who work through their unfinished business and settle down do not have to keep up the endless compulsion to join new fellowships. This is evident when we consider the marriage relationship. It is easy enough for us to see a problem in the individual who cannot find the right spouse and runs from relationship to relationship until he is fifty, never marrying because he has not found the "right one" or each person he dated had "too many issues." Decades of church hopping are little different, though we tend to be less critical of it.

---

1. Edwin H. Friedman, *Generation to Generation: Family Process in Church and Synagogue* (New York: The Guilford Press, 1985), 198.

UNMET NEEDS

Individuals from dysfunctional families often report feeling a void and an uncertainty over family relationships. Having never had supportive functional relationships of the kind we all yearn for (see chapter 7), these new believers often see in the church a chance to "re-family." Finally, the opportunity to get what they have never experienced looms in front of them. It is almost more than they can take in. They have a new Father and His representative, the pastor; a new family, the local church; and a new "me" with a new nature. One can almost hear the hallelujahs.

Though the church is like a family with fresh opportunities, counting on it to fulfill dreams of a perfect family may be a setup for disappointment. A newfound relationship with Christ and His church can provide a wonderful experience, but it cannot be expected to make up for the deficits one brings to salvation. Don't forget: The church itself is composed of imperfect people, all with their own hurts and unresolved issues.

Many times new believers do initially experience what they so desperately need and recovery begins. The church is healthy, accepts their hurting, and provides a place of recovery. Others experience a less positive scenario. In fact, their disappointment in their church experiences may be so severe that it leads to bewilderment and even greater despair. Often the only recourse they see is simply to look good on the outside and figure out their troubles as best they can on the inside. *Feelings are not important,* they say to themselves. *Just think straight, look sharp, and keep your failures a secret. Things probably aren't any better for anyone else.* Or so the thinking goes.

THE UNCERTAINTY

Since relationship skills are basically caught, not taught (though they can be enhanced by teaching), the new Christian sometimes feels lost. Knowing he should not repeat the patterns he experienced as a child and hearing about a new set of guidelines without ever having practiced them himself or seen them in practice, the new believer often feels inadequate, confused, and uncertain about what "normal" Christian relationships are all about.

One of the more common illustrations of this uncertainty has to do with the concept that Christian men are to be the "spiritual leaders" of their homes. Most men have never experienced that sort of godly leadership in their own homes as they were growing up. A man often feels successful if he can just numb the effect of some of the painful things inflicted upon him as a child. He's surviving, not thriving. Now he has a wife who, taking her cues from the pastor and women's Bible study leader, feels strongly that the hindrance to the development of Christlikeness in their home is his failure to be a spiritual leader. After all, she can't be responsible for that area. God has assigned that task to her husband.

But her husband is extremely uncertain about venturing into these uncharted waters. He has no idea if he is doing it right or even if he is on course. And he is not alone. If the truth be known, most evangelical men feel as though their spouses have much higher expectations of them as spiritual leaders than they can meet. They see their best efforts as paltry. So why try when you know you are going to fail? Add to this the fact that the husband can see all kinds of dysfunctional relationships in the church families around him, and it is no wonder he settles for a musty old role rather than a new fresh experience with God and others.

CHURCH FAMILY ROLES

People in a church tend to gravitate toward the same family roles they had in their families of origin. Add to that the encouragement the new believer receives to join an adult fellowship or small group, and you have all the external trappings of being important and belonging to a family.

It's a pretty good feeling when viewed from the exterior. Internally, however, little has changed. True, the roles given the new believer reassure him that he is important as an individual and that he belongs to the group. But, as explained in chapter 4, he has picked a church characterized by a relationship style already familiar to him and where he's likely to find a sense of security based on predictability. So it won't be surprising to find that pretty soon he's settled into a relationship role not too different from the one he had in his family of origin or the one he has in his own family.

The following four role categories are taken from recovery specialist

Claudia Black.[2] As you work your way through the descriptions of these categories, remember that the reassurance the roles provide the individual about his attachment to the group is what is important.

Overly Responsible Members

Each church has its overly responsible "children" who support it, lead it, and contribute to it, all following the "party line" with fatherly pastoral support. Statements such as "If only everybody could be like (person's name), wouldn't it be great?" abound. These individuals take it upon themselves to keep everybody happy, to do all the serving, and to anticipate ahead of time whatever needs to be fixed. In small churches, this role often is filled by the pastor's wife.

The only problem is that the role is never appreciated or noticed except through a departure or loss. It is just assumed that the overly responsible ones in the body will carry out their role. And, until these types leave or die (or have a heart attack), they will continue to do everything needed. Let's face it, healthy or not, this system works. But dues will be paid in the long run in terms of dysfunction and burnout.

Acting-out Members

These are the ones who continue to stay in the church family but who cannot live up to its codes of behavior and appearance. They are the members of whom it is said, "If it weren't for (person's name), we would be doing pretty well." This individual's "besetting sin" is the focus of the church family's prayer life and the talk among its members.

As in a dysfunctional family, acting-out members (or entire families) "act out" the church's pain. Their role is so necessary and ingrained that the more the church attempts to change their behavior, the worse they have to become. If they were well, and therefore "like everybody else," they would no longer be the object of everyone's concern, prayer life, and interest. They would lose their sense of specialness and belonging. And besides, the church body would lose the caretaking mission they have adopted.

2. Claudia Black, *It Will Never Happen to Me* (Center City, Minnesota: Hazelden, 2001), 11–26.

A strange twist can take place when healing does begin to occur. Because the acting-out role has such permanence in the life of the individual (or family) who adopts it, sometimes just as he begins to experience improvement, a crisis "happens" to come along to reassure him that things really have not changed after all and that his relationship to the church is still intact. In the same way troubled families resist change of any kind, the status quo in the church relationship is preferable to any change at all, even if that change leads to health.

Mascots

These are the loyal "pets" of the local church family. Everyone enjoys their presence, admires their personality, and keeps them locked into a role. Mascots are the ones who accept the responsibility for acting as though the family is functioning as it is supposed to. They don't do the necessary hard labor. That is not their task. Their responsibility is to make everybody feel good about belonging to the Lord's family. As in the dysfunctional family, these folks are often the center of everybody's attention and affection, while the hyper-responsible ones are killing themselves without recognition from anyone.

The Adjusting Members

These are the folks who move in and out of the church family, depending on how well it is going. If another church has a better program going, they move; if another preacher is saying what they want to hear, they go to listen. When things are good at the "home" church, they come. If things are not so good, they go elsewhere or just stay at home, much like the "adjusting child" who stays in her room, or practically lives at her friend's house, when things are rocky. Adjusting members are in and out of the church and not very committed, yet they are not so distant that they lose their membership, either.

Just as in the dysfunctional family, when any recovering member begins to respond in a new way, difficulties usually ensue. Many times the recovering member feels he needs to find a new church that will allow for the new identity and different relationship style he feels. When that happens, the "church family of origin" often feels abandoned or betrayed and senses a need to develop its own version of why the individual left. This version is often designed to protect the family image and to convey the idea that the *faithful stayed* while the *unfaithful strayed*.

FAMILY RULES AND CHURCH WORSHIP STYLES

Just as families do, churches practice the rules described in chapter 4: Don't talk, don't trust, don't feel.

Liturgical

Individuals who grew up in a family lacking trust (dependability and security) often seek out a church atmosphere that seems to make up that emotional deficit. In the liturgical worship style, the process is predictable. Everyone knows ahead of time what will happen during the service, and the service repeats itself week after week. For those growing up in chaos, confusion, and unpredictability, the liturgy is a haven, a safe place to relax, and they don't have to talk. They just attend, sit in their pews, are seen, and participate only when necessary.

Evangelistic

Just the opposite can be true for children who were to be seen and not heard. Children from families emphasizing the "don't talk" rule often gravitate to the evangelistic style of worship. Here they find encouragement to talk and are given the exact message to say. Many times this message is a formula, making it easy for them to express their feelings about spiritual subjects. Most times these churches are noisy with casual conversation. After all, the members now have the license to talk with their new family. The church becomes a gathering place, a key ingredient in the social structure binding these individuals together. Many times the new church family becomes so significant that it actually assumes greater importance to the individual than his family of origin.

Charismatic

Individuals whose family life acknowledged few of their feelings as children may find themselves attending charismatic fellowships. Emotional

expression has been denied them for so long that they find the experience of free expression offered by the charismatic church breathtaking.
It is all part of doing it differently, of finally having permission to express
themselves in ways they always knew they wanted to. Deep within them
rhythm and music always existed, but neither was tolerated in their family
of origin. Or maybe their daily lives were (and still are) so painful that they
yearn for a life pattern totally different from what they experience every
single day. Now the new family recognizes this free, expressive behavior
as normal and natural and actually makes it mandatory for attachment.
No wonder the church often holds more significance for these individuals
than their families of origin. They have found what all their lives they have
been searching for in a family.

Individuals with difficult backgrounds can often confuse good and bad
with stylistic preference, but we each have different tastes and different
needs. The sooner we acknowledge that, the less likely we will be to pro-
nounce as "wrong" somebody else's church preference.

EVANGELICAL CHURCH PERSONALITIES

Different churches will attract different kinds of parishioners and pastors.
Whereas a person enters his family of origin without any choice, he does
have a choice when he joins a local church. That choice has to be a mutually satisfying one, or long-term bonding cannot take place. Put another
way, the choice must be mutually satisfying in that he agrees to the rules
by which the new family practices family togetherness. But often uniden-
tified and unfinished family of origin patterns make the church a prime
area for the displacement of important and unresolved family issues.

This selection process helps a person clarify his relationship style and,
once identified, guarantees that the power base determining the church
family rules will remain unthreatened. *The dynamics of relationship styles
are so foundational that they are often at the root of church splits*, for church
splits nearly always occur over family rules and not family beliefs, as is
commonly assumed. Doctrine rarely splits a church anymore.

The amazing thing is that hundreds (often thousands) of church members in a local assembly tolerate even bizarre behavior, often for an unbe-

lievably long time. Overabundant loyalty and other factors common in troubled families cause individual church members to accept the unacceptable in church behavior, all of this under the guise of "being biblical" or "practicing New Testament Christianity."

Churches and families often mirror one another. Secrets, abuse, and immorality tolerated in the one can be practiced in the other. *Anything that can run in families can run in churches.* The pastor who lives in immorality will attract families who tolerate immorality. Similarly, abusive families will tolerate abusive church leadership.

Just like a family, church leadership often develops an official interpretation of the family patterns they practice. Secrets are ignored, and the church goes on, often with only a slight pause to detour around them. Just as a compass one degree off course on a long journey can lead to a destination miles from the desired original objective, so, too, can the collective detours around the secrets of the church and its member families take it places it would have never chosen to go in the beginning.

Questions for Reflection

1. What kind of church family have you chosen now? In the past? What do you foresee for the future?

2. Was your initial church family parallel to your family of origin, or the opposite of it? How long did you stay? Why? What did it take for you to leave? Was your departure parallel in any way to your other departures—from family of origin, initial marriage, job, school, and so on? What common patterns might be emerging?

3. How do you feel about the effort of this chapter to make our church family selection process more natural? For example, does this chapter generate in you misgivings as to whether God led you to your present church? What feelings does this chapter create in you? Does it make you feel more/less free, more/less responsible, more/less eager to stay? Does this chapter relieve you because the material makes sense?

4. What runs in your church family? Are there patterns in your church's history? Do you see balance in the lives of individuals who participate in your fellowship? What percentage of the members of your church stay there to stay away from something else?

5. Where do you fit in? What role do you play in your church family? Do you like that role? How does it compare with the role you had in your family of origin?

6. What do you think about the comments about husbands' uncertainty over wives' expectations for being the spiritual leader in their homes? Have you and your spouse talked about this issue? If not, try it.

PART THREE

FAMILY HEALTH: HOW TO DO IT RIGHT
WHEN YOU LEARNED IT WRONG

7

Learning to Bond

John Townsend

THE STORY is told of a little girl who, when frightened at night by noises in the dark, called out to her mother, "Mommy, Mommy, come here! I'm scared. There are big monsters in here!" The mother, not wanting to miss an opportunity to give a spiritual object lesson, replied, "Don't worry, honey, Jesus is there with you." After a moment of reflection, the little girl called back frantically, "But Mommy, I need someone with skin on!"

In this little vignette an important family principle unfolds that will be the guiding thought for this chapter: *The first and most fundamental human need the family should meet is the need for forming deep and loving attachments,* the need to develop the feeling of being close to someone "with skin on."

Family, by definition, is about relationships. However, many people assume that because they came from families whose members spent time together, attachment automatically occurred. In reality, nothing could be further from the truth. Many people report the sensation of being "alone in a crowd," of "not belonging," or of "not fitting in" as part of their everyday experience. This sort of experience reflects a basic lack in their ability to feel welcome and connected to others, or, put another way, reflects a lack in their sense of belonging. But what is "belonging," and how can we determine if belonging is an area of struggle in our lives? The following section gives us a working definition of the term.

WHAT IS "BONDING"?

A bond between two people is an emotional and personal investment they have in one another. It is a relationship in which all of the parts of the soul—feelings, needs, thoughts, values, beliefs, joys, and sorrows—are shared with and valued by another. The Bible shows us a picture of bonding in Jesus' description of His relationship to us, and ours to each other. He refers to it as "abiding":

> Abide in Me, and I in you. As the branch cannot bear fruit of itself unless it abides in the vine, so neither can you unless you abide in Me. I am the vine, you are the branches; he who abides in Me and I in him, he bears much fruit, for apart from Me you can do nothing. If anyone does not abide in Me, he is thrown away as a branch and dries up; and they gather them, and cast them into the fire and they are burned. If you abide in Me, and My words abide in you, ask whatever you wish, and it will be done for you. (John 15:4–7)

To abide is to live in, or remain in, relationship with someone else. When we bond and attach, our inner life abides in the life of another person.

When we are bonded, we "matter" to someone. When we are connected to another person, we feel that we make a difference to him, that our presence is desired when we are around and missed when we are absent. This sense of "mattering" is in direct contrast to feeling overlooked, forgotten, or even simply tolerated by others.

As designed by God, the family should be the very first place where its members can learn to count on the safe nurturance of others to fuel their emotional needs. It should be a "filling station" where needs for love are met so that its members have the strength to go out and interact with the world and take their place as people with purpose and mission. These needs for love and interaction are met through many sorts of experiences:

• Entering the world of the other person and actively listening to what he is saying.

- Understanding the members' needs and emotions and drawing them out, rather than staying on a "task" or "activity" level in all conversations.
- Making vulnerability and need a good thing in the family, so that it's okay to ask for comfort and support.
- Parents modeling vulnerability with each other, so that the kids can see how it's done.

THE PRIMACY OF BONDS IN THE FAMILY

Why are human attachments so important? Because God Himself is relational, and He designed us in His image to be relational. Relationship is the fuel of survival, growth, and success in the family.

A Biblical Perspective

The nature of God indicates how important bonding is. Consider the Trinity: God the Father, Son, and Spirit (Matthew 28:19; 2 Corinthians 13:14). The mystery of the connection of the three Persons of the Trinity models the truth that God by nature is in relationship. Because of His connectedness, God is free to love us, but He does not *need* us. He is, at all times, bonded to the other parts of the Trinity. He has taken care of His own relational needs.

Because we are made in His image, human beings are relational; we are in need of bonding. We are incomplete in isolation. Though Adam's creation was a "good" thing, it was "not good" for him to be alone (Genesis 2:18). God focuses on relationships, of which marriage is an example. Solomon warns, "Woe to the one who falls when there is not another to lift him up" (Ecclesiastes 4:10). Difficult times are made even harder when we go through them without attachments.

The New Testament teaching on the church emphasizes the basic need we have for connection with each other: "And the eye cannot say to the hand, 'I have no need of you'; or again the head to the feet, 'I have no need of you'" (1 Corinthians 12:21). For example, the little girl described at the beginning of this chapter was designed to reach out for "skin" when she encountered darkness and isolation.

Many Christians going through losses or trials have been unintentionally injured by well meaning friends who have told them, "Just trust God, and leave it with Him." This sort of advice denies the hurting person one of God's primary avenues of comfort and support: the incarnational healing of His Body on earth. God does not intend for us to struggle alone with our sorrow. He has specifically made a place in our hearts for Him and for His people. When one of those places is isolated or ignored, we suffer. We are the stewards of God's manifold grace (1 Peter 4:10). People are the delivery system of the grace of God.

Perspective from the Physical Universe

God's physical universe illustrates the primacy of the need for attachment. Consider the workings of plants, for example. A plant grows when the correct ingredients (food, water, air, sunlight, and soil) are provided. If one of these primary ingredients is denied, the plant wilts and begins to die. In addition, different parts of the plant need each other. Quite often, a family with bonding deficits sends its members out into the world "unnurtured" and thus unprepared for the demands of life. These people often feel rootless and lost as a result.

"I'm thirty-two, and I'm not going anywhere," said Sandra, who was seeing me for counseling about a sense of emptiness and depression. "All my friends are marrying and settling down, enjoying their careers and lives, and I can't even hold a job longer than six months. I don't know how to be close, or what I need in a relationship. I guess I just don't feel a part of the human race." Sandra's experience reflects a deep lack of belonging—a lack of bonding—in her life.

Perspective from Your Own Life Story

Consider for a moment your own life history. Think back over the hardest year of your life. Chances are that, whatever your circumstances, that year held some sort of relational loss or a season of extreme isolation from others. Even in the physical presence of others, many Christians carry the burden of a problem, secret, or loss that has never been shared with another "person with skin on."

"But you don't understand," Joan said to her counselor as she attempt-ed to grapple with a painful divorce, a troubled daughter, and job stress-es. "It's just not right to bother others with these problems. They've got problems of their own. Besides, I should be able to handle this by myself, shouldn't I?" Joan's life is rife with isolation: the aloneness of being a single parent coupled with the sense of being cut off from others who could help her in her struggle. No wonder she feels an almost unbearable burden.

If bonding is such a deep need in our hearts, what part does the family play in it? It is the place in which our "bondedness" is either developed or injured. God has made the family an incubator in which our sense of basic trust and dependency is formed in thousands of experiences over time. If we find that our emotional needs are welcome in the family, we will expe-rience a sense of bondedness throughout our lives. But if our emotional needs are not addressed or are met inconsistently, we will experience in-stead a feeling of aloneness and emptiness.

COMPONENTS OF FAMILY BONDING
Safety

Just as plants need protection from storms, disease, and deprivation, peo-ple need a place of emotional shelter. The family's job is to provide its members, especially its young children, a sense of unconditional cherish-ing. There should be an atmosphere of feeling "connected" no matter what conflicts exist. This is partially what Paul means in Ephesians 3:17 when he speaks of our being "rooted and grounded in love."

Have you ever noticed what an infant does when he or she is startled by a loud noise? Say an adult nearby sneezes suddenly. After an initial star-tled response, some infants will only require a few seconds of holding and comforting before they relax again. Other babies will require several min-utes of calming by a parent before they regain their equilibrium. What makes the two groups respond differently?

Often the different response derives from the number of consistent, predictably loving experiences the parents have given to the child. The baby who feels safe recovers quickly because he has a foundation of safe memories on which to draw. The baby who feels unsafe is shaky and ungrounded for a long time because he is deficient in that store of safe memories. The experience of the first child is parallel to that of the man in Luke 6:48 who built his house upon a rock. The "flood occurred, the torrent burst," but the house could not be shaken "because it had been well built." The child whose life rests upon a solid foundation of love will enjoy a sense of safety as he journeys through life.

Safety in the family also means that:

- the parents give their children the assurance that they are loved by Mom and Dad no matter what they do or say.
- family members reinforce vulnerability among themselves by taking the initiative to ask about each others' feelings.
- the parents are consistent in their behavior and promises; the children know their family is a predictably safe environment, not a chaotic or confusing one.
- the family makes anger and sadness acceptable as part of the vocabulary of its conversation.
- the parents understand the roots of conflicts before taking action to punish them.
- family members are emotionally warm and gentle when hurt feelings are expressed.

Unfortunately, many people find deficits existed in the emotional safety of their original families. These deficits likely showed up in one of two forms, as *emotional withdrawal*, in which the children learned that expressing their needs and feelings resulted in a parent detaching from them, or as *emotional attack*, in which the children learned that expressing their needs and feelings caused a parent to become emotionally or physically hostile. Both of these reactions will seriously undermine a child's ability to feel secure in who he is.

Modeling
The second component of the bonded family is the ability of the parents to "teach by doing" through being vulnerable with their joys, sorrows, and

conflicts. When children hear Mom and Dad sharing hurts, losses, and fail-ures, they learn that feelings and needs are normal parts of life. Children will learn best from their own parents how to confess problems and solve them in a family, although they must be discreet, since children pick up on their parents' emotional needs. God is an example of a parent who shared His losses, as when Jesus wept over lost Jerusalem (Luke 19:41–44).

A lack of modeling in the family tends to cause the members of that family to regard their feelings as bad or weak. Children, especially, will assume that if their parents don't talk about their struggles or emotions, they must not have any problems. One woman expressed it this way: "When my father died, there was no warning beforehand, and no griev-ing afterward on my mother's part. It was as if a TV channel had been switched: One day he was here, one day he was not. And since I never saw her sadness and anguish, I figured the feelings I experienced were bad and inappropriate. The shame I felt over my emotions was overwhelming."

Note the "double tragedy" here: Not only did this woman feel unsafe with her grief, but the lack of modeling by her mother also provided no "picture" from which she could learn what the season of mourning de-scribed in Ecclesiastes 3:4 actually looks like. The result was a feeling of badness and shame.

Emotional Openness

This third component is at the heart of bonding. Whereas safety provides a place for bonding, and modeling offers object lessons, the ability to com-municate our needs and struggles in an environment of receptivity and trust is the essence of family attachment. Table 7.1 diagrams deepening levels of emotional openness among people. As you study the table, try to pinpoint your family's predominant level of intimacy.

Let's observe a few things about these differing levels of closeness. First, one level is not worse than another; instead, different levels meet dif-ferent needs. We need relationships on all five levels. Jesus loved the world, but He had twelve deep relationships, the disciples. And of that dozen, three—Peter, James, and John—were chosen to be closer friends. Of those three, John was recognized as being "the disciple whom Jesus loved" (John

TABLE 7.1

Levels of Intimacy

LEVEL 5:

The most intimate level of sharing; members discuss their thoughts and feelings about each other.

LEVEL 4:

Deepening friendship; members discuss their thoughts and feelings about their struggles, fears, and anxieties.

LEVEL 3:

Friendship; members discuss their emotions about certain subjects.

LEVEL 2:

Beginning of friendship; members report their opinions and thoughts about events but not their feelings.

LEVEL 1:

Acquaintances; members report events with no opinions or emotions connected. Sports, weather, and news are permissible topics of conversation.

21:20). So we need and enjoy casual acquaintances as a means of relaxing, but at the same time experience a sense of internal isolation and emptiness if our family never addresses issues deeper than current events.

Second, as the levels of bonding increase, the number of relationships at each level decreases. In other words, we can have many acquaintances, but only a few truly deep bonds. Why is this? Simply because it takes an incredible amount of time, many shared experiences, a good deal of work, and solid commitment if we are to take a relationship to the fifth level of intimacy. We should consider ourselves blessed if we can count a handful of these closest relationships by the end of our lives. Jesus' pattern of human relationships demonstrates this reality.

The second point brings us to the third: Because the family is the incubator where bonding is learned, the quality of the years spent in our family of origin determines, to a large extent, our predominant level of intimacy in subsequent, adult relationships. That is not to say that this level is set in stone forever. But it is helpful to see that our relational problems have origins. Detached families often tend to produce detached children.

The bottom line is that our struggles have roots. True, we are all sinners, being born of Adam. There is indeed a generational component to our sinfulness. But the types and kinds of problems we have tend as well to be a reaction to our most important relationships: those within our families of origin.

SYMPTOMS OF BONDING DEFICITS

Bonding deficits reveal themselves in characteristic ways. Look through the following checklist of signs that a family is having difficulty in achieving closeness. As you read the list, ask yourself: Do any of these symptoms characterize my present family, my family of origin, or both?

- Whenever all of the members of the family are at home, they spend all of their time in different rooms.
- When the members of the family need comfort, they turn to food, drugs, work, hobbies, or other non-relational substitutes.
- Conversations in the home center around *what* a person is doing as opposed to *how* he is doing.

• Relationships outside the home take precedence over relationships inside the home.

Individual family members may also experience symptoms that point to a problem in bonding:
- Feelings of isolation
- Loss of meaning
- Substance abuse
- Shallow relationships
- Depression
- Obsessions with activity or work
- Suicidal thoughts or actions

What Do the Symptoms Mean?

If you have experienced some of these symptoms in your family of origin or your present family, consider the symptoms a red flag signaling that something has gone wrong. Jesus said, "Every good tree bears good fruit; but the bad tree bears bad fruit" (Matthew 7:17). In other words, use the symptoms list to help you understand the bonding problem.

The symptoms tell us that when love and closeness are absent, the family has no firm roots upon which to build everything else. When Dad loses his job he will not think of his home as a safe place to refuel before launching out to find another job. When Ryan feels shut out by the peer group at his new school, he will isolate himself in his room and listen to music instead of coming to dinner with everyone else and sharing his hurt. When Debbie's boyfriend breaks up with her, she will hide her loneliness and sadness in a binge of overeating but not share with the rest of her family the hurt that caused the overeating.

DEVALUATION AS A RESPONSE TO FEAR OF INTIMACY

Let's suppose you have been able to identify several symptoms of bonding deficits in your family. Often, in order to survive the sense of loneliness and emptiness brought on by bonding deficits, individuals develop barriers to intimacy that soothe the pain but prevent the problem from being resolved. These barriers can be described in one word: devaluation, or undervaluing our need for close, loving relationships.

We don't come out of the womb devaluing love. On the contrary, we are born empty, frightened, needy beings. We want love. But after repeatedly being punished for having needs, seeing others withdraw from our needs, and having our trust betrayed, most of us inwardly decide that numbness is the best policy: *To protect myself, I must live without needing others. And to live without needing others, I must not feel my own needs.* Devaluing our needs has the personal usefulness of protecting us from the pain of needing care and grace from others and not being able to have it. There is no more excruciating emotional pain in the world than this.

The problem is that this protective device (called a coping style in chapter 4) becomes a prison. Devaluation of the people who didn't bond properly with us generalizes to a habit of withdrawing from anyone who has something to offer. As a result, we increase our isolation. Paul addresses this self-induced isolation in 2 Corinthians 6:11–13 when he speaks of a lack of love returned: "Our mouth has spoken freely to you, O Corinthians, our heart is opened wide. You are not restrained by us, but you are restrained in your own affections. Now in a like exchange—I speak as to children—open wide to us also." I find Paul's reference to children particularly significant, since we tend to learn this prison-making behavior early in life.

We can see this defense mechanism in action in Phil, whose wife had left him. "I think you guys have it all wrong," Phil protested to his concerned friends. "I'm really fine," he continued. "She wasn't that great a wife anyway, and I really didn't love her. It's no great loss." Not until several months later, when Phil developed a severe drinking problem, did the lie (devaluation) became apparent.

Certainly even some of our closest relationships can be unsatisfying at times. In addition, feelings of love are mercurial. It is normal for one sinner to have a hard time constantly feeling close to another sinner! But did you notice Phil's devaluation of how important his wife was to him? He used it to protect himself from the anguish of his loss.

DEVALUATION AS A WAY OF EXPLAINING OUR WITHDRAWAL

While devaluation of our need for others is often a response to a fear of attachment, other kinds of devaluation come about as a means of explaining and justifying our withdrawal. These devaluations revolve around the three primary relationships we have: with God, with others, and with ourselves. Consider the following devaluating statements:

Devaluations about God:
"God isn't trustworthy since He allowed me to be badly hurt."
"God doesn't care about me personally."
"God is more concerned about what I do than who I am inside."

Devaluations about others:
"People can't be trusted."
"There is no one who truly cares about my needs."
"If I am vulnerable, I will be hurt."

Devaluations about ourselves:
"I have no need for others; I am fine alone."
"Closeness is an illusion."
"I am too bad to be loved."
"It is wrong and selfish for me to ask for comfort."

Observe that most of these beliefs have a kernel of truth to them. The statement "I am too bad to be loved" is certainly true in the sense that all of us are sinful. All of us carry guilt in our soul that testifies to our sinfulness. But there is also much to love in each of us. The lie is that our eligibility for love depends on our performance, and often a completely perfect performance at that. Phil conveniently used his wife's human imperfection (the kernel of truth) to devalue her importance to him (the lie).

The problem is that these beliefs generally develop from experiences at an early age and then graduate from truths within the dysfunctional family to truths about the universe. What was once a way to protect us from further hurt becomes an isolating wall around our hearts, sealing us off from the grace of God and His body, the church.

UNDERSTANDING MY BONDING DEFICITS

We have seen God's ideal for family bonding and what can go wrong. Now let's turn to personal situations and learn about what may have gone wrong. Take time to examine how your past affects your present:

1. A Personal Inventory

In prayer, ask God to help you have insight into your own struggles with intimacy: "Search me, O God, and know my heart; Try me and know my anxious thoughts" (Psalm 139:23). Look through this chapter, and note which parts of the discussion relate to your life.

2. List of Symptoms

Begin with the behaviors, attitudes, and feelings that trouble you most. Do these aspects of your life point to isolation? Are they substitutes for attachment to others?

3. Underlying Problems

In this section of the inventory, deal directly with your experience of isolation. Do you find that you struggle with devaluations of love? What sort of thoughts do you find recurring that tend to push away your need for closeness?

4. Causes of Bonding Deficits

Evaluate your family of origin's ability to bond (i.e., its capacity to provide safety, modeling, and levels of openness). Was the family emotionally cold? Was there instead a pseudo-intimacy that masked isolation? Was emotional vulnerability met by indifference, hostility, anxiety, or withdrawal?

5. Linking Past to Present

Take a look at how you may be repeating the isolating patterns you learned in your original family. Do you expect inconsistency in those you are close to? Are you afraid to trust because you expect to be let down, betrayed, attacked, or made to feel guilty?

SKILLS FOR REPAIRING BONDING DEFICITS

The last section dealt with exploring the bad news of past injuries. You made it through, so good for you! The following section will deal with the good news: God wants to help you heal. Your ability to connect emotionally with others is like a torn or injured muscle. It may be atrophied and undeveloped, but it can be repaired and strengthened. Here are some ways you can restore this God-given "muscle."

1. *Find a safe, uncritical relationship* (or two) in which you can share emotions at a deep level and begin to bond. This relationship may be with your spouse, a friend, a pastor, or a counselor. Just remember that bonding wilts in the face of detachment or criticism but flowers in the presence of acceptance and warmth.

2. *Become aware of your resistance to intimacy.* Do you withdraw when you find yourself becoming needy? Do you find yourself devaluing relationships when you are hurt?

3. *Take risks with emotional issues.* Are there experiences, memories, thoughts, or feelings you have never shared with anyone? Allow someone to care about this isolated and unloved part of yourself. James 5:16 says, "Confess your sins to one another ... so that you may be healed." In the context of this chapter the verse might be paraphrased, "Confess your lacks to one another ... so that you may be healed."

4. *Allow yourself to feel the need for closeness.* Allow yourself to need uncritical relationships and to be comforted by them. Jesus said, "Blessed are those who mourn, for they shall be comforted" (Matthew 5:4).

5. *Pray on a personal level* rather than a grocery list level. In other words, share your feelings and responses using "I" statements in your prayer, such as, "Lord, I also feel very alone in this experience."

6. *Meditate on who God is* rather than simply on what He does.

7. *Begin to forgive your family* for injuring your "bonding muscle." Forgiveness is a process and takes a great deal of healing to accomplish. Beginning at this step brings you further out of the bondage of repeating the negative patterns you learned there. Remember, your parents were probably also injured by their parents!

8. *Allow for mistakes.* Practicing bonding means sometimes getting hurt when we attempt to be close, and sometimes even withdrawing when we need to get close. But we learn by mistakes. Hebrews 5:14 states that "solid food is for the mature, who because of *practice* have their senses trained to discern good and evil" (italics added). With practice, we learn who is safe and who isn't. With practice, we learn the skill of taking emotional risks. And with practice, we begin to receive and give what God has intended for us from the beginning: ourselves.

ARE YOU A "BONDING CASUALTY"?

As this chapter on family bonding closes, you may have identified yourself as a bonding casualty. You may feel that your life is typified by emotional isolation. And if you have experienced deficits in the bonding patterns of your original family, you may also feel some sense of confusion about bonding or tend to trivialize the need for finding close relationships. That is normal and is due to a tendency to be frightened of intimacy ("being") and more at ease with activities ("doing").

Carl was struggling with family bonding problems. He had begun to experience deep feelings of sadness about some major losses in his life. After wrestling with his painful emotions, he decided to phone his counselor. Taking the initiative by calling his therapist after hours was highly significant because it was the first time in his life that he had ever *asked for* a personal connection to share his pain. Carl poured out his sadness and feelings of loss, then asked for advice on what to do with his emotional pain. He expected his counselor to suggest some kind of action like "get more organized, put it behind you, do something positive." But the therapist told him, "Carl, you're doing what you need to do."

It gradually dawned on Carl that during the lengthy conversation, his pain had been understood and shared. In making an intimate connection with his counselor, he felt immense emotional relief.

In seeking the healing God wants to provide for bonding deficits, we need to learn the lesson of simply allowing others to care about us without performing; we need to be Marys instead of Marthas (Luke 10:38–42).

Is this an easy task? No! In fact, it will probably be one of the most difficult tasks you will ever encounter, especially if you suffer from bonding difficulties.

As you begin the process of learning bonding, ask God to direct you to safe, attaching, forgiving people. No one can repair this injury in a vacuum. God made people a part of the process. As you search for those few people with whom you can begin to learn to trust, look in your church, your social circles, your work, and your family. Ask yourself, *Would he or she be gentle with or critical of my emotions? Would I be understood, or would I be judged?* Then, after careful and prayerful evaluation, take a risk—a small one, but a risk nonetheless—and let yourself be vulnerable with that person.

Questions for Reflection

1. In which of the three components of bonding (safety, modeling, and openness) have I experienced problems? How has this affected my life?

2. What activities, good or bad, do I find myself substituting for intimacy?

3. When are my bonding injuries most painfully apparent to me (social situations, alone at night, and so on)? Use these times as a barometer of your spiritual and emotional well-being. As you identify the situations in which you become most aware of bonding deficits, ask God to reveal ways of relating that will help you make it through the tough times (for example, calling a friend, taking a risk to share feelings, or honestly discussing your needs with God in prayer).

4. Who is the person in my life right now with whom it would be the safest to begin a vulnerable relationship?

5. Which of the bonding skills can I begin to learn this week? What would be a first step in building this skill?

8

Learning to Set Boundaries

John Townsend

A YOUNG MOTHER confided tearfully to a friend that she had been having problems with her eighteen-month-old son. "We've been so close ever since he was born, but now it seems so hard. He disobeys and disagrees with me. I miss my 'easy baby.' I guess we're entering the 'terrible twos.'"

The woman's friend responded, "I can understand your frustration, but I see this stage differently. I call it the 'terrific twos.' I love to see my child's personality emerge and begin to blossom."

What a radical difference in the child-rearing perspectives of the two women! The first wishes her baby was once again compliant and cuddly and resents the stubborn willfulness of her child. The second sees the child's emerging energy as a joy. Their conversation illustrates a problem many people have about what a "good baby" and a "bad baby" are. Passive, obedient, cooperative babies get the white hats; those who are more self-directed and oppositional ("strong-willed" children) get the black hats.

And yet it is this "willfulness" that helps set the stage for the second developmental need designed by God to be nurtured in the family: the need for *separateness*.[1]

---

1. For further treatment of boundaries and separateness, refer to titles by Cloud and Townsend in Appendix B.

OUR NEED FOR SEPARATENESS

To understand separateness, let's return to *bonding*, the developmental need mentioned in the last chapter. Many people consider themselves "people persons" who are able to bond and connect with others. Yet these same people often feel overwhelmed, anxious, and frustrated about the obligations and responsibilities their bonded relationships seem to demand. The reason for this is that bonding alone is not enough. We also need self-ownership—self-determination of what we are to do with our lives and resources. In a phrase, we need stewardship over how we use our lives (Matthew 25:14–30).

A good example of bonding without separateness is found in a man in his mid-thirties I'll call Kevin. He began seeing a counselor for symptoms of depression. As Kevin explored his life and circumstances, he began to notice a pattern in his important relationships. "All my life I've been so afraid to disappoint people that I've never said no to anyone," he said. "In order not to let down my family, my wife, my boss, and my friends, I've worked later, longer, and harder than anyone I know. I even feel that God depends on me for everything. And I'm so busy taking care of everyone else's requests for my time that I've been ignoring my own needs. No wonder I've felt burned out for years."

Kevin began to recognize the source of his problem with separateness. He had come from a family where differences of opinion were seen as rebellion and where compliance was rewarded. This injury to his will manifested itself in Kevin's adult life as chronic depression.

How do mistreatments of the will lead to depression? When we don't feel free to be honest and truthful with others about our opinions and values, we set in motion the process of allowing ourselves to be controlled by the feelings and desires of others. That in turn leads to a deep sense of powerlessness and resentment, based on a feeling of helplessness. If this sense of powerlessness and resentment is not checked, one's hope of being in normal control of one's life begins to die. Depression is the result of the death of hope. Proverbs 13:12 says, "Hope deferred makes the heart sick." When we feel constantly owned and controlled by others, our hearts suffer.

BLOCKS TO BONDING

The interrelationship between bonding and boundaries is shown in table 8.1.

TABLE 8.1
Interrelationship of the Capacity to Bond and the Capacity to Set Boundaries

BONDING	HIGH	LOW
BOUNDARIES HIGH	Block 1 INTIMACY	Block 3 ISOLATION
BOUNDARIES LOW	Block 2 FUSION	Block 4 CHAOS

The value across the top, "Bonding," represents the presence or absence of deep attachments in a person's life. The value at the left of the chart, "Boundaries," represents the presence or absence of clear separateness and autonomy. The results that occur when these elements are combined are listed inside the four blocks. Let's examine each of the blocks in turn. Give some thought to which pattern, if any, applies to your life.

Block 1

Block 1, "Intimacy," indicates that *closeness plus clear separateness produces a healthy intimacy.* In such a relationship differences of opinion and even arguments do not disturb the sense of being "rooted and grounded in love" (Ephesians 3:17).

In counseling, Mary began to grasp the deep relational conflicts underlying her condition. "I've always feared that differences between me and *anybody* would cause me to be abandoned forever, whether it was my husband, my children, or even the paper boy. Working so hard to avoid conflict burned me out. Now I can 'speak the truth in love' and still feel connected to people I disagree with."

What was the epochal "truth telling" event that made all the difference for Mary? Simply that when a staff member invited her to a field trip to the beach, she declined because she wanted to do some reading. When the staff member, to whom Mary felt close, did not become angry or hurt and reject her over her choice, Mary actually wept in surprised relief! Having a relationship in which differences of opinion or desire didn't result in rejection was something she'd never experienced in her childhood family.

Block 2

Block 2, "Fusion," indicates what happens when bonding without boundaries occurs. One or both people in a relationship are unable to be free and separate. In fused relationships, differences of opinion and normal degrees of conflict are either denied or punished. We described a fused parent-child relationship in chapter 2 in the relationship of Isaac and his mother, Sarah. Fused relationships among adults can also be seen in the suffocating heat of romantic infatuation, when romantic partners do not know where one person starts and the other ends. The couple is "lost" in love for one another. Their relationship is fused, which is in large part why such relationships are usually rocky, unfruitful, and short-lived.

Block 3

Block 3, "Isolation," shows what happens when boundaries exist but not bonding. An isolated individual may be very much in charge of life and have a well-developed ability to say no but at the same time not have any deep emotional relationships. People in this pattern tend to "die on the vine," withering from a lack of normal interaction and love. We saw in chapter 1 how David's son Absalom felt isolated from his father. Absalom thought it was necessary to do drastic things to get his father's attention, such as setting a wheat field on fire. The workaholic or loner is a modern-day example of this type.

Block 4

Block 4, "Chaos," describes the relational capacity of a person who is injured in both attachment (bonding) and separateness (boundaries). He feels lost in relation to others and to himself. He is neither connected nor self-directed, but is in a spiritual and relational limbo.

Those in this category are the most injured; for them both connectedness (the basis for feeling loved) and self-responsibility (the basis for self-control) are at low-functioning levels. Today we see many adolescents with these two deficits. They are unable to form deep attachments and have extreme problems in delaying gratification and being responsible for themselves. It is no wonder drugs have become so prevalent in our culture, with their promise of helping the user to feel loved (connectedness) and to experience instant gratification (a result of having weak boundaries, which form the basis for self-control).

BOUNDARIES: THE SEPARATENESS TOOL

Given that we need both attachment and freedom, how does this second ability, the ability to be separate, develop in the family?

The family was designed by God to not only help us connect emotionally, but to help protect us against harm, and to help us make good choices. The mechanism for building our wills is called a *boundary*. What we mean by the term *boundary* is that which distinguishes one person from another. It is that which sets him apart. Just as we can tell property lines of ownership by legal boundaries, in the same way spiritual and emotional boundaries exist to show us what is "mine" and what is "not mine."

Our skin is a boundary. It keeps us separate from others. It keeps bad things out (infections, dust, and germs) and good things in (our organs, muscles, and so on).

The word *no* is a boundary. When we say "no," we are keeping something out, perhaps an unwanted obligation or a demand on our time or money that would be debilitating. When we use the word *no* skillfully and without fear or guilt, we help to define and protect ourselves. Using *no* is like developing a muscle. The skill improves with practice. The "no muscle" takes a great deal of time to mature, and it is susceptible to injury, particularly as we are growing up in our families of origin.

This doesn't mean we shouldn't help others or give to them. The Bible teaches that love is part of our lives (Mark 12:31; 2 Corinthians 9:7; 1 John 3:16). But it also teaches that there are times we are to say "no" as well (Psalm 101; Proverbs 4:23).

PROPERTY LINES, KNAPSACKS, AND BOULDERS

If we look at boundaries as spiritual "property lines," we can see that boundaries determine what we *are* responsible for and what we are *not* responsible for. God has made us responsible for those things, and only those things, that are within our boundaries. We encounter conflicts with ourselves and with others when we make one (or both) of the following mistakes:

- not taking care of the things within our boundaries or
- taking care of the things outside our boundaries

Galatians 6 is a good chapter to study in connection with this point. There Paul asserts that "each one shall bear his own load" (v. 5). The Greek word for "load" means *knapsack,* or what we carry daily on our journey through life. It is the same "burden" that Jesus spoke of when He said, "My yoke is easy, and my burden is light" (Matthew 11:30 KJV). This "load" comprises that responsibility we should shoulder for ourselves.

Our individual knapsacks contain things like our attitudes, opinions, beliefs, needs, choices, feelings, values, time, possessions, money, gifts, talents, behavior, and bodies. We are to set limits around these parts of our lives and protect and maintain them *ourselves.* It is our responsibility to care for them.

The converse is also true. Just as we are positively to take care of the elements of our lives that are properly within our own boundaries, so we are to refrain from taking care of the things that are inside other persons' boundaries. If we fail to observe this restraint, two negative results are likely to take place:

- We will sabotage the spiritual growth of another person (Ephesians 4:15) and
- We will neglect our own God-given responsibilities and become poor stewards of ourselves (Matthew 25:14–30).

The important thing about our knapsacks is that they are part of our lives and are our burden. In other words, we should not "carry" (take responsibility for) someone else's knapsack. God Himself doesn't do that. For example, God allows people to refuse His gift of salvation. Think of Jesus' words in Luke 13:34: "O Jerusalem, Jerusalem, the city that kills the prophets and stones those sent to her! How often I wanted to gather your children together, just as a hen gathers her brood under her wings, and you would not have it!"

Just as Jesus allows others to make destructive decisions for themselves, so we have to accept the reality that we aren't strong enough, nor do we have the right, to take responsibility for others. We are to love them but not to parent them (unless we are legally responsible for them, as in parent-child relationships). When one adult "parents" another (even when the two adults are related), co-dependent, dysfunctional relationships almost always follow.

In contrast to our knapsacks, Paul describes a different "load" in verse 2 of Galatians 6. This Greek term is the word for *boulders:* heavy, crushing burdens that cannot be borne alone. These are the tragedies, crises, and losses that befall us, and they are not our fault. As best we can, we are to help one another with these boulders. Sharing these burdens is practically the definition of brotherly love and pleases God greatly.

God wants us to make a clear distinction: to handle boulders differently from knapsacks. While we can only love, but not take responsibility for, someone whose knapsack is giving him problems, it is entirely proper for the body of Christ to surround the stricken, crushed member with caring and support until he or she can get back on their feet.

The story of the Good Samaritan illustrates this perfectly (Luke 10:30–37). The Samaritan, finding the injured man, didn't put him up in a hotel for the rest of his life. Instead, he provided enough funds for the man to be healed and assumed that after an appropriate time he'd be on his way. The Samaritan loved the wounded man but did not take permanent responsibility for him. To do so would have been to deny the injured man his own identity and autonomy.

Paul is saying in Galatians that we are fully responsible *for* ourselves (bearing our knapsacks) but only partially responsible *to* others (helping them with their boulders when we are able). Put another way, God's plan for growing up involves taking full responsibility for our lives and helping others in crisis, but we are not responsible for the normal loads of others (i.e., their knapsacks).

We hurt ourselves and others if we shoulder the wrong load. If we try to pick up their boulders instead of our knapsacks, we will end up denying others their adulthood and prevent them from learning that their actions have consequences. We will make them dependent on us and ourselves codependent with them.

THE FAMILY AND BOUNDARIES

The second great function of the family, after bonding, is to help its members take responsibility for their "loads" by setting boundaries and developing the ability to make wise and responsible choices.

How does the family provide this need? These are some of the ways:

- by allowing family members to state their opinions
- by making it safe to disagree without fear of criticism, rejection, or isolation
- by encouraging members to think for themselves
- by helping members discover and train themselves to use their unique gifts and abilities
- by allowing anger to be expressed appropriately (Ephesians 4:26)
- by setting limits with consequences, not guilt or fear
- by respecting each other's "no" choices
- by allowing age-appropriate choices:
    - condition of a bedroom (a disaster or well-kept)
    - choice of relationships

– development of Christian values

– how to spend money

– when to be with friends instead of family

The family has a tricky job: It needs to keep members intimately attached yet simultaneously separate.

What Goes Wrong?

Many Christian families do not produce members who can set limits with others. What happens in these families that impairs the growth of the "no muscle," thus hindering the development of healthy boundaries?

Basically, parents who are confused about boundaries tend to produce children who are confused about boundaries. There are several source points of this confusion, some of which are given below:

- Parents who feel abandoned when their children begin to make autonomous choices. These parents respond to autonomy in their children by conveying guilt or shame about their lack of love and loyalty to the family or to the parents.
- Parents who feel threatened by their increasing loss of control over their children. These parents use anger or criticism, not guilt or shame messages, to convey their unhappiness over the children's newfound separateness.
- Families that equate disagreement with sin.
- Families that are afraid of the anger of their children.
- Families that are hostile toward the anger of their children.
- Families that praise compliance in the name of togetherness over healthy independence.
- Families in which emotional, physical, and sexual abuse occur. These kinds of abuse cause severe damage to the children's sense of ownership of their bodies and themselves.
- Families in which the children feel responsible for the happiness of the parents.
- Families that rescue children from experiencing the consequences of their behavior.

- Families that are inconsistent in limit-setting with the children.
- Families that continue to take responsibility for the children in adulthood.

Let me illustrate the parent who feels abandoned by her child's autonomy. Cynthia was a wife and mother of two who could not understand why she felt a growing, gradual sense of isolation that increased as her children grew older. Finally, in therapy for depression, she began to realize she was feeling abandoned by her children as they became more and more autonomous. "But why in the world would my kids' growth make me feel lonely?" she asked.

Digging deeper, she began to see that her mother had made her the center of her life. If Cynthia was around to support her, Mom was happy. But if Cynthia wanted to spend time away from home with friends, Mom became sad and depressed.

When Cynthia married and moved out of state, her mother began isolating herself, developing physical problems, and making sure that all letters and phone conversations to Cynthia focused on how empty life was without her. Those messages were like a knife in Cynthia's heart, full of guilt and shame messages about what a neglectful daughter she was.

Cynthia's mother felt abandoned because she made Cynthia responsible to take care of her loneliness instead of developing her own adult friendships. As a result, Cynthia was conflicted about her own autonomy. Her boundaries were fuzzy. This pattern was repeated in Cynthia's own family when she married and had children. She held similar feelings toward her own children that her mother had felt toward her. There was an essential difference, however: Cynthia wanted the family pattern stopped in her generation and worked hard to allow her kids age-appropriate freedom without making them feel responsible for her loneliness. She wanted to halt the cycle of transmission (discussed in chapter 4) so that healthy patterns might be sent down the line instead of the unhealthy ones. As we can see, where the family makes the child (1) responsible for what is not his, and/or (2) not responsible for what is his, boundary injuries ensue. Note that we say boundary "injuries" and not simply "confusions."

Errors in this area actually do harm to a developing human being. Just as some people suffer from untreated childhood physical injuries well into adult years (for example, unset broken bones or untreated tooth decay), many Christians take boundary injuries into their mature years so that the deficits affect life, love, and work functions. Jesus taught that good trees produce good fruit and bad trees make bad fruit (Matthew 7:16–20). In the same way, clear family teaching and experiences on boundaries help create healthy boundaries for the child. The reverse is true as well.

What Is the Result?

When a family has not provided clear "ownership" guidelines to its children, the children learn to say "yes" to what is not theirs (yes to the bad) and "no" to what is theirs (no to the good). Although some families produce children with one or the other pattern, many more families produce children who live out both extremes.

Laura was seeing a therapist after her third marriage ended. "I'm hopeless," she said. "I always end up with the same type of man: charming, flashy, and totally irresponsible. Am I a magnet for these losers?"

Laura's latest failure had come about when she found that her husband of three years was having an affair (in addition to being chronically unable to hold down a job for more than a few months). She had been the stable breadwinner in all three marriages. Was she a magnet?

In a way, yes. Both of Laura's parents had been alcoholics, loving in their intentions but perpetually inconsistent in following up on their promises. Laura had painful memories of being left at school without a ride, of meals she had to make herself, and of promises of gifts that never materialized and special events that never occurred.

Yet Laura had never learned that this pattern was not her fault but her parents'. In one counseling session she remarked, "I figured they didn't follow through because I wasn't being good enough, so I became better than good. I became the most responsible kid in the world."

Then the responsible little girl entered adulthood. Typically, when these types of conflicts are not noticed and worked through, there is a repetition of the pattern in the next generation, and that happened in Laura's case. She married men like her parents, who "talked their talk" but didn't "walk their walk."

Why? She put it together one day: "I've been trying to *fix* these men with my love, the way I *couldn't* fix Mom and Dad." She had developed a hallmark symptom of codependent relationships, the need to "fix" other adults.

Laura is an example of someone who had been trained by her environment to allow irresponsible people into her life, thinking their irresponsibility was hers to repair. Put in our boundary discussion terms, she had learned to say "yes" to the bad.

It's sad. Think of all the mature, reliable, consistent men who had possibly been interested in Laura but in whom she was not interested. There was nothing to fix in their lives! Laura was not only saying "yes" to the bad; she was also saying "no" to the good.

RESULTS OF BOUNDARY PROBLEMS

Table 8.2 illustrates the types of boundary problems individuals contend with, both in relation to themselves and to others. Perhaps you'll see yourself, elements of yourself, or your loved ones in this diagram.

TABLE 8.2
Boundary Problems

	CAN'T SAY	CAN'T HEAR
"NO"	Block 1 FEELS GUILTY AND/OR CONTROLLED BY OTHERS	Block 3 WANTS OTHERS TO TAKE RESPONSIBILITY FOR HIM
"YES"	Block 2 SELF-ABSORBED; DOESN'T RESPOND TO OTHERS' NEEDS	Block 4 CAN'T RECEIVE CARING FROM OTHERS

Block 1

Block 1 represents the person who can't say "no" to others because of guilt, fear, or an excessive desire to please. This person gives up stewardship of his life to the control of others' wishes, needs, and demands. Though he is active in helping others, the inability he has in setting personal limits often causes him intense confusion, anxiety, and frustration because of a lack of direction. Kevin, cited earlier as a workaholic who didn't want to disappoint anyone, fit into this category. In contrast, God warns us against "seeking the favor of men" too much (Galatians 1:10) but rather urges us to make pleasing Him the number one priority in our lives.

Block 2

Block 2 refers to the individual who does not respond to others' boulders, the "excessive loads" of Galatians 6:2. He does not say "yes" to valid needs of others. His behavior is in direct contrast to the pattern exhorted in Proverbs 3:27: "Do not withhold good from those to whom it is due, when it is in your power [note the condition here] to do it." The characteristic neglect of caring reflected by persons in this category usually derives from one of two causes:

- a critical spirit toward others' needs (Pharisaism)
- a self-absorption in one's own desires and needs to the point of excluding others

It is important here not to confuse self-absorption with a God-given sense of taking care of one's own needs first so that one is then able to love others.

Whereas Blocks 1 and 4 have to do with the codependent person, Blocks 2 and 3 have to do with the dependent person, the one who takes little responsibility for his own life but instead seeks to make others bear the load. Dependent people tend to gravitate toward codependents, because a codependent's lack of proper boundaries is likely to cause him to neglect himself and "rescue" the dependent individual. That is what had happened to Kevin. He had a dependent mother, wife, and boss, and he could not care for all of them and himself, too. The result was depression and burnout. Laura illustrates the other half of the equation. She consistently found dependent types to marry so that she, in her codependence, could rescue them.

Block 3

Whereas Block 1 refers to the person who can't *say* "no," Block 3 refers to the person who can't *hear* "no." People with this boundary problem tend to project responsibility for their lives onto others and, either through manipulation or demand, get others to carry the load God intended for them alone. These people generally have not had consistent limits set for them by their families and so tend to exploit others to get their needs met, thus violating the boundaries of others. They have extreme difficulty in taking ownership for their actions, indeed for their whole lives.

Roger grew up in a well-to-do family in which all normal responsibilities had been taken care of by his parents or the hired help. He had never held a summer job, nor had he been held accountable to make good grades in school. After a few months of marriage, his wife was amazed to find he had run up thousands of dollars of credit card purchases and was writing bad checks. When she angrily confronted him over it, he said resentfully, "Don't worry; someone will take care of it."

That someone had always been his parents, who, because of their own boundary conflicts, had acted as Roger's financial safety net. They took responsibility for things inside Roger's boundary. He had always assumed someone would absorb the consequences of his actions, but that someone was never him. Now Roger's inability to delay gratification was causing him to violate his wife's financial boundaries. He couldn't hear "no" from her regarding his excesses.

God sees a situation like this quite differently from the way Roger did. He has ordained a law of the universe we informally call the "law of sowing and reaping." Responsibility brings success; irresponsibility brings failure. As Paul wrote in 2 Thessalonians 3:10, "If anyone is not willing to work, then he is not to eat, either." An empty stomach would quickly help teach Roger to respect his wife's boundaries more!

Block 4

Block 4 refers to the person who denies God-given needs because of guilt, a desire to please others (Colossians 3:22–23), or a fear of emotional abandonment. This is a matter of setting boundaries where none should be. The person believes it's not okay to have needs, whereas in actuality no such barrier or boundary exists. This category includes people who have difficulty in being direct with others about their needs for comfort, support, encouragement, and caring.

People in Block 4 usually fall into two groups:

- those who are afraid of, or feel guilty about, asking for what they need (in contrast to Jesus' encouragement in Luke 11:9 to "ask," "seek," and "knock") and/or
- those who are unaware they have emotional, spiritual, or relational needs (in contrast to Jesus' blessing in Matthew 5:6 on those who "hunger and thirst for righteousness, for they shall be satisfied")

The people who fall simultaneously into Blocks 1 and 4 are considered codependent. They take responsibility for others' needs but neglect their own. And, yes, it seems that Kevin, our people-pleasing workaholic, fits both blocks himself. Kevin was much more attuned and sensitive to what others wanted from him than attuned to his own needs for his own growth.

The boundary confusion these people suffer is technically known as a "reversal," since there *are* boundaries where there should not be any, but *no* boundaries where there should be some. The condition can lead to workaholism, depression, eating disorders, substance abuse, and panic attacks.

OBSTACLES TO TAKING OWNERSHIP

The heart of the problem of ownership is responsibility, determining what is and is not mine. It is failing to take appropriate ownership within appropriate boundaries. Part of what hinders us from doing so is a reliance on myths about God, others, and ourselves:

Boundary confusion about God:
- God should always say "yes" to me

- God is responsible to keep me from suffering loss, whether or not I take responsibility for my life
- God expects me to love Him and others without being responsible for my own legitimate needs

Boundary confusion about others:
- If I say "no" to others, I'm being selfish
- I am indispensable to the needs of others
- My happiness is the responsibility of someone else in my life

Boundary confusion about ourselves:
- If I am needy, I am bad
- If I love, I should be loved in return
- My life is not my responsibility

Fundamental to these myths is confusion about the relationship of love and limits. Many families operate on the unspoken assumption that love and limits are antagonistic. One wife told her husband tearfully, "You never provide enough money for us to have traveling vacations. If you really loved me and the family, you'd do something about it." Yet at this point, the husband was trying to work their way out of severe debt problems, and it was tough going.

Why did the wife fail to see that? Because she interpreted her husband's appropriate limits (i.e., "no fancy vacations until we're out of debt") as an absence of love, while in reality it was healthy responsibility. Strange though it may seem, often those with firm, healthy boundaries are characterized by others with unhealthy boundaries as being selfish, uncaring, or unloving. The frequency of such instances indicates how far we as a society have strayed from God's healthy design.

People who have good boundaries tend to be the most loving people in the world. Why? Because they don't give from obligation or fear but as "cheerful givers" (2 Corinthians 9:7). Loving, affectionate people need to develop firm boundaries, and firm people need to show love. That is growth into the image of God.

ATTITUDES TO ADOPT AND ACTIONS TO TAKE TO REPAIR BOUNDARIES

By now you may feel overwhelmed with regard to setting proper boundaries, especially if you grew up with unclear or inappropriate ones. But take heart; there is hope for repair. If you have been injured in your ability to set or respect boundaries, steps are available to repair this broken part of your soul. What follows is a suggested plan.

1. *Make a personal inventory.* Begin by looking at the fruit, or symptoms, in your life. Here is a partial list of signs of boundary problems:

- feelings of obligation
- hidden anger/resentment toward others' demands
- inability to be direct and honest
- people-pleasing
- life out of control
- no sense of identity or "who I am"
- inability to fulfill work demands
- blaming others or circumstances too much
- excusing/denying failure
- depression
- anxiety
- compulsive behavior (eating, substance abuse, sex, money)
- chronic conflictual relationships

2. *Categorize underlying problems.* Refer to table 8.2, and ask yourself: Which blocks identify my struggles? Do I say "no" to good things and "yes" to bad things? Do I have difficulty respecting others' boundaries and/or hearing their needs?

3. *Research causes.* Think about your family of origin. It will tend to contain the roots of the problem. Go over the items listed in the subsection titled "What Goes Wrong?" Ask yourself: Did I come from a family in which I was responsible for my parents' happiness? Was I not given enough limits or responsibility for my life? Was my family so close that no one could set

limits? As you identify the roots of the problem, begin to trace the line between patterns in your childhood family and your present struggles.

4. *Link past to present.* Answer yourself: How am I repeating in my present relationships the boundary problems of my family of origin? In answering, look at your present family, work, social, and church relationships. Be specific.

5. *Determine goals for repair.* Ask yourself these questions as you refer to table 8.2:

Block 1: Do I need to learn to set boundaries for myself with others? Do I need a "no muscle"?

Block 2: Do I need to be open to others' needs, after I've been a good steward of myself?

Block 3: Do I need to learn to respect others' boundaries? Do I need to hear "no" better?

Block 4: Do I need to learn to ask directly for what I need? Do I need to learn the difference between stewardship and selfishness?

6. *Evaluate your resources.* You will need the following to repair boundary deficits:

(a) *A willingness to understand God's boundaries as a model.* Study God's dealing with Paul in 2 Corinthians 12:7–9. Paul repeatedly asked God to deliver him from an affliction. The affliction was obviously painful, either physically or emotionally, for Paul called it a "thorn in the flesh." Yet God held His boundaries with Paul by refusing to deliver him because He had something else in mind (a lesson in humility for Paul).

Not only is God able to say "no," He also has boundaries against running over the wills of others. The story of the rich young ruler in Matthew 19:16–26 offers a good place to meditate on this point. After observing that the ruler worshiped money, Jesus challenged him to give up his god and follow Him. But when the ruler went away grieved (because he was unwilling to part with his money), Jesus allowed him to leave. He didn't negotiate with him or say, "How about 90 percent?" God allows non-Christians to leave Him; He gives believers choices. He knows that we will grow only if we can make sound choices for which we are responsible.

(b) *A relationship with one or more people who will help you set healthy boundaries.* Those relationships should incorporate accountability and unconditional acceptance of your being "unfinished."

Find out if your church has support groups or small group Bible studies with an emphasis on "truthing and loving." Ask the leaders, "Is this a group in which people give loving feedback to each other?" That's the sort of group you'll need, as opposed to an intellectual study or a "critical parenting" style of group. If an appropriate support group is not available, find a Christian counselor who understands boundary problems; if you need to, ask the counselor if he or she knows of local Christian groups where people work on repairing their boundaries.

(c) *Time.* Allow yourself time to repair your boundaries. Developing appropriate boundaries is a skill involving much practice with relationships. You won't accomplish it overnight.

7. *Practice setting your boundaries.*
- List the areas of your life over which you are a steward. Which areas do you handle well? Which poorly?
- *Practice saying or hearing "no" in your safe relationships.* For example, when your best friend or spouse asks, "Where do you want to eat dinner?" don't just shrug and say, "Doesn't matter to me." Take a risk and say (if that is how you feel), "I really don't want to go to the restaurant you picked. How about this one?"
- Notice when you tend to be dishonest about your needs or those of others.
- *Practice setting small boundaries before you tackle large ones.* If you have never said "no" before, start with something less crucial than putting your job on the line. Say "no," for example, to picking up after your son or daughter (or someone else you tend to pick up after).

• Expect resentment from those who are not accustomed to your newly set boundaries. Jesus warned, "Woe to you when all men speak well of you, for their fathers used to treat the false prophets in the same way" (Luke 6:26). Why were the false prophets tolerated? Because they said what others wanted to hear. The true prophets of God of the Old Testament rarely won popularity awards. Why not? Because they were truth-tellers. Their truth sometimes rocked the boat.

There may be people in your life who "love" you simply because you don't disagree with them. If so, when you decide to begin "truthing" in your expression of opinions, values, and emotions, and "truthing" in your behavior, these people may resent the fact that they are suddenly in relationship with another will besides their own. If that occurs, you may need to rely on your support group while you work on establishing appropriate boundaries in the problem relationships.

BE ENCOURAGED: YOU CAN MEND BROKEN BOUNDARIES

Working through these steps in the power of the Holy Spirit, given the right relationships, wisdom, practice, and time, will help you repair boundary problems caused by a troubled family. God wants you to be able to protect yourself from evil and to choose good things for yourself. He knows that when you have developed this capacity you will also have developed the capacity to be a "good and faithful" servant (Matthew 25:21), taking care of the life and the self He has entrusted to you.

Questions for Reflection

1. How do boundary problems relate to the symptoms I listed in the personal inventory given in this chapter?

2. As I identify how my family of origin contributed to my boundary deficits, can I commit to begin the process of forgiving them?

3. What myths keep me from resolving boundary confusions?

4. What is my greatest fear about setting limits with others?

5. How am I not taking care of my knapsack? How am I trying to take care of someone else's knapsack?

6. In which of my relationships (other than my relationship to God) would it be the safest to begin discussing my problems with boundaries? Can I talk to this person this week about the subject?

9

Learning about Goodness/Badness

Henry Cloud

THE WHITNEYS had "the ideal Christian family." They were an intact family unit: two non-divorced parents and three children. Mr. Whitney, a deacon in his church, earned a respectable living as a professional. The family lived in a nice neighborhood and had a lovely home, the modern version of the "white picket fence."

The children were doing well, also. They excelled in school and in extracurricular activities. They had accomplished everything their parents and the community expected of them, with the exception of fourteen-year-old Derrick, the "black sheep" of the family. But all in all, the Whitneys were the perfect Christian family; at least they thought so. And everyone on the outside thought so, too.

But inside the walls of the house and inside the "walls" of each person, things were not so perfect, although no one in the family ever talked about it.

Though he was relatively placid at work and in other settings outside the home, in the family setting Mr. Whitney was given to outbursts of rage when things did not go just the way he expected them to. Likewise, Mrs. Whitney was sullen and disappointed when her children did not live up to her expectations. As a result, the children keenly felt as if they were hurting their mother when they "failed."

Also, they were beset by a fear of failure and a constant drive to do better, but they knew enough not to reveal their imperfections and negative feelings to their parents or to family friends. Shameful things like imperfections and negative emotions were never to be shown outside the home. After all, "What would people think?" So went the Whitney family code.

For many years the Whitneys kept the praises of church and community coming, even if they lived behind a façade. And for a long time it worked. Then Susan, the sixteen-year-old, came down with anorexia nervosa, a severe eating disorder. She tried to hide it and so did the family, but one day she collapsed in church from sheer weakness.

The Whitneys could no longer hide their secret. Now the whole church knew, and word began to spread outside the assembly to the community. Mr. Whitney began to get inquiries at his workplace, and Mrs. Whitney began to sense unspoken questions from her acquaintances. Their family doctor told them that anorexia nervosa was a life-threatening condition and that they had better get Susan to a psychiatrist at once or risk her life. Mr. and Mrs. Whitney realized they had a serious and inescapable problem on their hands.

What had gone wrong? After all, hadn't they built the ideal Christian home?

IDEAL?

When we look at the basic needs a person has that should be met in the family, a foundational principle often gets overlooked: *The family is the place where we learn how to deal with failure, where we learn about being less-than-perfect beings in a less-than-perfect world.* There is no ideal person, no ideal world (short of heaven), and therefore no ideal family. When a family pretends it is ideal, or when it believes that it must be ideal, serious problems ensue.

When God created the first family, Adam and Eve, this problem did not exist. Adam and Eve lived in a perfect world and were perfect beings. For a time, they lived out the ideal. They were not even to know anything different: "But from the tree of the knowledge of good and evil you shall not eat" (Genesis 2:17). Their task was simply to go on being perfect and not even know that they were! That's true humility! But as we all know, they ate the forbidden fruit, and we have been aware of good and evil ever since.

It is hard enough to live in a world of good and evil. But it is even harder to live in such a world without any way of dealing with it. Yet that is precisely what the "ideal" family tries to do. It tries to insist that good and evil are not both present in the home. As a result it has no provisions for dealing with reality.

The Bible tells us that if we call ourselves ideal, we are liars (1 John 1:8). It recognizes our desire for the ideal, however, and says that we even long for it (Romans 8:22–23). It also provides us with ways of dealing with the coexistence of good and evil, and that is what every healthy family does. It gives the members of the family a safe place where they can learn what the ideal standards are, try to reach them, realize they fall short, learn how to deal with those disappointments, practice becoming better, and still be "real" and authentic throughout the process.

We will look at ways a family can make itself a safe place for less-than-perfect people to learn the skills to help them live in a less-than-perfect world. If you came from a troubled family, you probably did not feel safety where badness, failure, and evil were concerned, and as an adult child from a less-than-perfect family you are probably still a bit shaky on the matter. The goal of this chapter is to help you acquire the understanding and skills you did not develop at home.

THE "LESS-THAN-PERFECT" PARTS

We know that after Eden, our natures acquired less-than-perfect parts, but what does that mean? Here are some of those less-than-perfect parts.

Feelings

As real people living in a real world, we are going to have some negative feelings, such as sadness, anger, and fear. In addition, we are going to have some "fallen" sorts of feelings as well: jealousy, envy, pride, rage, lust, and so on. Every person has all of these feelings at some time in his life (Mark 7:21–22). That's a given. The family needs to be a place where its members are given the skills they need to deal with the less-than-perfect parts of their personalities and to find safe solutions for these deficiencies. We need to learn that it's okay to have less-than-perfect emotions, and that our family will help us to resolve them.

Attitudes

We do not always have godly attitudes. The Bible says that our hearts are often out of line with reality and the ways of God (Ecclesiastes 9:3; Romans 3:23). Children do not come into the world with godly attitudes. They need to be taught how to face squarely the ungodly attitudes they do have and how to grow out of them. If the family is a place where children must deny their bad attitudes and always look good on the outside, they will never learn to deal with those attitudes. They will become "whitewashed tombs," to use Jesus' words (Matthew 23:27). If the family continues to suppress the reality of those internal bad attitudes, the children will become hardened and emotionally impenetrable, hardly godly personality traits.

Behaviors

The Bible tells us we are less than perfect in our behavior. It is amazing how often the Bible tells us that we can be expected to sin (Romans 3:23). Sin is part of our nature, but parents often act surprised when they have children who are sinners. We all fail in our behavior, and if we did not learn in our childhood families how to face our bad behavior honestly and to respond to the natural consequences of that behavior, we are in real trouble. We will either have to deny our behavior or stay stuck in it, neither of which is God's wish for us (Romans 6:1–2).

DYSFUNCTIONAL WAYS OF DEALING WITH BADNESS

Now that we know that the ideal family is a fantasy and that the ideal world has been lost (as has the ideal person), we can consider some of the ways dysfunctional families deal with badness.

Pretend the Bad Isn't There

An old illustration in the family therapy community illustrates this strategy. A family has an elephant living full-time in the house. It has become part of the family. But no one in the family says anything about it. Family members watch TV between the elephant's legs, they vacuum around its massive body, they silently pick up the mess when he rummages through the leftovers on the dinner table. They ignore the eight-ton elephant and go on being a family as if there were nothing wrong.

But after a while the elephant begins to smell, and his natural habits cause other problems. Pretty soon the elephant can be denied no more. He *lives* there.

The family has realized the problem too late, though. The carpeting is ruined, flies and maggots have infested the house, the city is about to serve a condemnation notice, and myriad other problems are snowballing. They have a first-class crisis on their hands.

Comical as this story may be, it illustrates the way many problems are treated in a dysfunctional family. They are simply denied. An unspoken rule about badness seems to be in operation: *We will pretend it just isn't there.* As with the elephant, badness is stepped around, ignored, not talked about. And, also like the elephant, it begins to smell and cause serious problems.

Maybe the elephant is Dad's drinking problem, or Mom's pouting, or Derrick's behavior problems, or Susan's depression and isolation. Possibly it is Dad's verbal or physical abuse of the children, which can't be faced because he is "such a good Christian man." Maybe it is Derrick's inability to make friends, which is difficult to see because Mom and Dad want to believe he really is popular at school. Perhaps it is Susie's inability in academics, which is denied because Mother has a master's degree in education and all of her children surely ought to be high achievers.

Or maybe the "elephant" is the ordinary sort of negative feelings everyone has. When anyone feels sad or angry, those negative experiences are pushed under the rug. Negative feelings are smaller elephants and more easily hidden than big elephants like alcoholism.

Whatever the "bad" thing that is denied, it will cause problems if it is not dealt with. The family may think there shouldn't be negative things in their house, but the Bible affirms that negatives do exist in this fallen world. Like the elephant, these negatives must be dealt with honestly and correctly. Sell the elephant to the circus, but deal with badness or sin in the family according to God's plan.

Pretend the Good Isn't There

Some families deal with badness by denying the good. They may do this in two ways: deny the ideal standard or deny the genuine good in an individual. Both strategies lead to serious problems.

When a family denies the ideal standard, it makes no attempt to achieve God's ideals. We have said before that it is a fantasy to believe that we can achieve all of God's ideals in this life, but that does not mean it is wrong for a family to try to uphold those standards or for family members to try to reach their potential (Philippians 3:14–16). God's standards provide us direction in our feelings, attitudes, and behavior, and if a family denies that those standards exist, it will drift rudderless and plagued by chaos. The children will have to find their way alone, and the parents will not be effective models.

In such families there is little teaching and correction when badness appears. Badness is allowed to be present as if there were no better way to be. Standards are not upheld. Maybe Dad's drinking is seen, but it is not called sin. Maybe Mom's extreme moodiness is accepted, but no one ever mentions that moodiness is not the best way to get one's needs met. Maybe the children's failures are never measured against the norms of other kids their age. They are allowed continually to make the same mistakes and not press on to anything better, even though they might be capable of good work. Or perhaps the parents do not strive to be the best they can be in various areas, and sloppy work is what they model for the children, with no value placed on excellence. They do not show the stewardship value the Bible exhorts: to make the most of whatever talent we have (Matthew 25:14–27). God's good standard is not there, and consequently there is nothing against which anything—behaviors or feelings or actions—can be measured.

The second way of denying the good is by discounting what is genuinely good in an individual and characterizing him as all bad. All of us have heard the saying "being on somebody's bad side," and that occurs in a lot of families. The child is on the parent's "bad side" and is unable to get around to a "good side." He is labeled "bad," whether the thought is spoken or unspoken. His strengths and good points are never recognized or acknowledged.

When this sort of labeling occurs, the child can grow up with extreme self-image problems, seeing himself as "all bad" whenever he fails or is less than perfect in his performance. He will call himself "stupid" and write himself off. He is unable to realize that even when he fails, he still has good points. Labeling of this kind often takes place in overly rigid, legalistic theological systems, whether a family system or a denominational system. In such settings, the inherent value of persons created in the image of God is ignored.

Children raised in such settings carry another disability: They cannot work out natural conflicts with others. When "all bad" thinking is modeled, the child grows up seeing others' failures the same way. Whenever anyone fails him in any way, he sees that person as all bad and writes him off the same way his dysfunctional family wrote him off. He grows up leaving friends, jobs, and spouses whenever he finds any degree of badness present, for all he can see is the bad. He has learned to deny the good, so in his mind there is no reason to continue in the relationship, job, or marriage. This sort of all-or-nothing thinking causes many broken relationships and prevents the development of conflict-resolution skills, an ability that is sorely needed in today's society.

Condemnation and Judgment

A third way of dealing with the elephant is to shoot it. Attack and condemn the less-than-ideal whenever it appears! In this mode badness is not denied but is simply condemned, along with the person doing the bad things. This approach evidences a complete lack of grace. No forgiveness is available to the transgressor. The strategy of condemnation and judgment carries the sense of the Old Testament law, which is described in the New Testament as merciless: "For whoever keeps the whole law and yet stumbles in one point, he has become guilty of all" (James 2:10).

Many people as adults struggle with the effects of growing up in families with this attitude toward badness. Their parents followed the motto "If you can't join 'em, beat 'em!" They would not allow themselves to reveal that they, too, were struggling, imperfect beings like their kids, so they beat the children (physically or emotionally) whenever their imperfections showed up.

If the parents heard feelings that were not perfect, they condemned the child. If they heard a bad attitude, they attacked and judged the child. If there was a failure in the child's behavior, they screamed at the child and angrily disciplined him. They lived out the unmerciful law, which is a far cry from the way the Bible talks about dealing with badness. Condemnation is not the way of the cross (Romans 3:20–24).

When people come from families in which there was a good deal of condemnation, they struggle with guilt and shame. They feel as if their failures can never be accepted and forgiven. Grace is a foreign concept, and it is difficult and sometimes impossible for them to feel and experience it. No amount of Bible study or encouragement to have their sins forgiven will sink into their damaged emotions.

These individuals are caught in the "guilt-sin cycle." They fail in some area, face all sorts of internal condemnation for the failure, and then feel unable to resolve the conflict. They interpret the crushing guilt as "conviction" and try to repent and commit themselves to do better. But since they have not resolved the causes of the behavior, they repeat it again and feel even worse. Sometimes, as their sense of guilt increases, they even run to the sinful behavior "just to feel better." That only increases their sense of guilt, and the cycle of compulsive behavior continues. "Who will set me free from the body of this death?" writes Paul (Romans 7:24). In fact, much of Romans 7 is devoted to this cycle.

THE BIBLE'S VIEW OF DEALING WITH THE LESS-THAN-PERFECT PARTS: GRACE: NO CONDEMNATION

The Bible's way of handling our less-than-perfect parts is grace, or lack of condemnation (Romans 8:1). Our less-than-godly feelings, attitudes, and behavior are measured in the light of the grace of God. The believer is totally accepted and forgiven in Christ while he is still in an imperfect state. He has what the Bible calls a "standing" in grace (Romans 5:2).

Many people do not know how this standing in grace feels because their family of origin has not modeled the forgiveness and acceptance. They have not experienced it in a real-life setting. The Bible speaks of two ways of "knowing." One is through learned information; the other is through experience. Many Christians "know" about grace intellectually, but their key learning experiences in their formative years were very different from the grace they read about in the Bible. Therefore, it is hard for their hearts to "experience" something they only "know" in their heads.

I recall a minister we'll call Carl, who participated in group therapy. Carl was struggling with a sexual addiction. Even though his training had prepared him to "know" in his head that God had forgiven him in Christ, his family-of-origin experience had him always "feeling" condemned. When his feeling of being a "bad" person reached its peak, he would succumb to pornography or prostitutes. Then he would feel worse! The cycle seemed impossible to break.

In the group we continued to express our unconditional love and acceptance of Carl, even when he slipped into such behavior. It dumbfounded him to have the group members express such unconditional love, and one day he blurted out, "I don't deserve your love. I don't deserve God's love."

To which we replied, "You're right. You don't. But you've got it anyway."

At that point in his recovery Carl began to make real progress. The simple experience of unconditional love began to change his life. He found that no matter what he did, he couldn't escape our love for him. That's grace—unmerited favor—for you. It can change anyone's life. And it should be present in every family.

It is important to see how the grace approach is different from other ways of dealing with badness. First, it does not deny our sin. The book of Romans, which is all about our standing in grace and our justification from our badness, begins with three entire chapters on sin. There is no realization of grace if our sin is not seen. Thus denial of the elephant is not present in this strategy. The failures, the bad feelings, the ungodly attitudes, and so on, are all identified for what they are. They are seen realistically and not denied; the difference is that the person is still accepted with love. He is shown kindness (Romans 2:4; Ephesians 4:32).

Second, in addition to not denying the presence of badness, the grace answer affirms our value, for we are created in the likeness of God. It does not say that we are "all bad" and worthless. It just says that our attempts at perfection are worthless. The Bible continually affirms the worth of man

(Psalm 8:4–6; Matthew 6:26), and in a healthy family the worth of each individual is continually affirmed, even in failure. No one should ever be seen as worthless or all bad.

Finally, the grace solution never condemns or uses anger as a way to point out failure. The entire New Testament conveys the thought that God is free from anger and condemnation toward us when we are cleansed through the sacrifice of Jesus (Romans 5:1). The biblically based family deals with imperfection the same way and communicates safety and acceptance to its members. It creates an atmosphere in which badness, worth, and acceptance are not denied. Badness is called what it is, but the value of the person is affirmed through love. Loving arms are put around him in the midst of his failure. Many adults who are still coping with hurts from their childhood families would give anything to have grown up in such an atmosphere! They find that being good does not equal value. Value comes from being loved.

"FAILURE IS NOT ALWAYS FAILURE"

Many times in Christian circles and families, there is further confusion about the nature of failure. Many families lack a realistic or balanced view of failure by expecting perfection, but another element that parents must take into account in monitoring their children's progress is immaturity.

Immaturity occurs when someone has not had the time or resources to achieve a level of growth that would enable him to perform in a certain way. God has established a path of growth for children so that they become adults as part of a process. There are specific stages and steps in the process of gaining adulthood. If someone has not attained a certain stage, he will be unable to perform what is required at that level (1 Corinthians 13:11; Hebrews 5:12–14). Time is required for growth (Ecclesiastes 3:1–8), but many parents seem blind to this reality.

In many dysfunctional families, children are required to be more mature than they are, and their age-appropriate immaturity is not accepted. They grow up expecting themselves to be further along than they are, with the result that they are prone to interpret their present state as failure. Think about it: living with the constant thought that your present condition is always unacceptable, no matter what age you are. What a prison! Yet it's a reality for millions who grew up in confusing families like these.

Unable is an unfamiliar word to these children. They live in a world of *shoulds*. They "should" be able to do this and that, even though they are not yet "big" enough. Imagine a little girl learning some new skill, such as cleaning up after painting. With all good intentions, she may put a dripping wet paintbrush into the silverware drawer. She may get a response from her parent, "You stupid idiot! Don't put that in that drawer!" But how was she supposed to know for the first time that the brushes didn't go there? She was just learning!

This happens frequently to baby Christians when others do not understand the stages of faith development (1 John 2:12–14) and expect too much of them spiritually. Older believers sometimes expect new believers, who have not yet been rooted and grounded in love, to display more fruit than they are able to display. This is common with addicts who begin to recover and then slip back into old habits. One slip does not a recovery invalidate! To a certain extent, we should expect a three-steps-forward/ two-steps-back pattern from baby Christians.

When adults from painful original families become Christians, they carry with them into their new family, the family of God, this inability to allow for immaturity. They constantly feel like spiritual failures and compare themselves to other believers with different gifts and backgrounds, instead of accepting themselves where they are at a particular moment, however immature (1 Corinthians 12:29–30; Galatians 6:4). It is easy to forget the "author and perfecter" of our faith, who has promised to bring us to maturity (Hebrews 12:2).

It is important for adult children of troubled families to realize that a strategy of not allowing for immaturity was probably present in their upbringing and to fight against it. They need to work on accepting immaturity as a part of the growth process and to accept themselves where they are at any given stage.

That does not rule out pressing on toward maturity; of course they will want to do that. It does mean adults in recovery need to realize that growth is a process and there will always be areas in which they will need to be stronger before they are *able* to do what they *want* to do. They will have to remind themselves constantly that an occasional spiritual failure does not mean they are bad, but rather means they are still immature and "in process." Continually condemning themselves is like someone scolding a toddler for spilling his milk. The little guy is just learning; give him a break!

THE FAMILY AND BADNESS

We saw in chapter 8 how tricky it can be to establish healthy boundaries in the family. Dealing with badness is not easy, either. But it can help everyone to grow into adulthood and to reach their potential as Christians and as people. We all need to learn how to deal with our imperfections and failures and at the same time hold on to ideals.

What goes wrong?

As we have seen, dysfunctional families deal with badness in hurtful ways. Let's look at a list of typical responses:

- the family acts as if someone is perfect and ignores that individual's badness
- the family idealizes one child, thus making him feel inappropriately important and the other children inadequate
- the family labels one child the "black sheep"; that child becomes the "container" for all the badness in the family
- when someone fails, the family ridicules him, making him feel ashamed of who he is
- when someone fails, the family condemns him and responds angrily to his failure
- the family emphasizes how it looks to others outside the family, thus creating the belief that image is more important than being honest and real
- there is a hush-hush attitude toward failure, weakness, or immaturity; imperfection is thus ignored and implied to be worse than it is; consequently, fear develops
- the family holds up impossible standards and does not value where a person really is in his or her process of maturity

- the family compares members to one another and to other people outside the home in a futile search for the ideal; no one is -good enough as he is
- there is no understanding that everyone has strengths and weaknesses and that having strengths and weaknesses is okay
- the idealized member acts as though he is too good for the rest of the family; he may complain about being "stuck with such a bunch of losers"
- sometimes all of these dynamics get "spiritualized" and the person feels these dysfunctional perspectives come from God Himself

PROBLEMS

People who grow up in families that deal with failure and badness in dysfunctional ways exhibit a host of symptoms. Let's look at some of them:

"The All-Good Me"

This person cannot admit she fails, is immature, or is sinful in her feelings, attitudes, and behavior. She sees herself as ideal and cannot own anything negative. She drives other people crazy, for obvious reasons.

"The All-Bad Me"

Some people reach this state when they fail, have a negative feeling, or realize some immaturity and cannot tolerate it. They have no grace inside to stand the failure and so immediately go into a state of all badness.

Depression

People who cannot feel okay when they discover negative aspects of themselves are prone to feelings of depression. They also are depressed because they cannot deal with the negative emotions of anger and sadness, both of which contribute to depression.

Anxiety

People who feel they have to be perfect are likely to feel a good deal of anxiety. They are always afraid they are going to fail or be discovered for who they really are: fallible human beings.

Perfectionism

Perfectionism obviously has a lot to do with an inability to deal with badness. A perfectionist cannot stand to find that any aspect of himself, others, or the world around him is not perfect. He can make life for himself and those around him miserable by his compulsive insistence on perfection in everything.

Enabling or Codependency

Many codependent people are codependent because they have never had permission to face and confront bad things about people they love. They feel they must help to hide the bad parts in themselves and others. The codependent helps others cover up their problems by making excuses for them, taking responsibility from them, and carrying loads that others should carry. They excuse sinful behavior and enable it to continue, thinking that they are being "forgiving" or "longsuffering."

Dissatisfaction

Many people have not been able to find satisfaction in a less-than-perfect world. They are always seeking the elusive ideal, and as a result, nothing is ever good enough. This strategy practically guarantees unhappiness in life.

Fear of Failure and Risk

Because their families did not teach them to tolerate and work with failure, many people are afraid to take new risks and therefore miss out on important opportunities to learn. They are stuck where they are in life, because change is too scary.

WHY DO WE DO IT THIS WAY?

If all these incorrect ways of coping with life are not helpful, why don't we just do it right? Oh, if it were that easy! The truth is that we learned a great many confusing things in our families of origin, and those confusions block our ability to work with our failures. Those confusions are in the same three categories discussed in chapters 7 and 8:

Confusion about God:

- God thinks I am all bad.
- God hates me for my failures and will punish me angrily; His grace does not apply to me.
- God expects me to be further along than I am able to be at this time; He forgets that sanctification is a process.
- God doesn't care much about my getting better.

Confusion about others:

- If I show my failures to others, they will reject me as my family did.
- If I show my sinfulness to others, they will think I am horrible.
- If I ask others for help with my shortcomings, they will think something is wrong with me.
- If others see my "badness" or mistakes they will get angry at me.
- Others have it "all together."

Confusion about ourselves:

- If I am not perfect, I am worse than everyone else.
- If I am immature, something is wrong with me.
- If I fail, I am defective.
- If I am unable, there is no hope for me.

A FUNDAMENTAL MISUNDERSTANDING

Fundamental to all these confusions is a misunderstanding about the true nature of man and the true nature of God. The Bible teaches that all humans have strengths and weaknesses and that all people will, at times, fail. In addition, it teaches that God is a God of grace and truth; He is One who will face our imperfections squarely, forgive us, and help us to do better. His Word says that we all sin, that we will be forgiven freely if we seek it, and that He will cleanse us totally (1 John 1:8–9).

The problem is that in the dysfunctional family, we learn to hide. This hiding began with Adam and Eve in the garden when they first became aware that they were no longer perfect. They hid (Genesis 3:7–10), and we all have been doing it ever since.

The problem with hiding is this: *Nothing can grow in the dark.* The apostle John talks about walking in the light and says that through a confessional process the broken parts in our lives can be restored to righteousness (1 John 1:1–9). James says the same thing: "Confess your sins to one another, and pray for one another so that you may be healed" (James 5:16). This is basically what happens in any good support group or therapy group, or in a good small group in a church setting: There is real confession.

FIGHTING BACK: ATTITUDES AND ACTIVITIES TO DEAL WITH IMPERFECTION

Let's look at some specific things a family can do to help its members accept their badness, failure, and immaturity, while at the same time promoting growth:

- Creating a grace-giving atmosphere where confession of any failure is accepted.
- When a member fails, loving him in his failure and not withholding love from him.
- Parents modeling an acceptance of their imperfections instead of acting as though they are perfect.
- Parents helping to make failures something to be learned from instead of condemning the child for those failures.
- Not being afraid to point out imperfection when it appears; calling it what it is and not participating in the denial game.
- Creating an atmosphere where everyone can talk about his negative feelings, attitudes, and behaviors and can find help for those negative areas without being scolded.
- Allowing family members to express negative emotions appropriately.
- Not allowing any member of the family to be seen as perfect.
- Affirming the value and worth of each person in whatever state of maturity he is.
- Making confession a lifestyle instead of a legal, punitive thing that only criminals do.
- Pointing out the strengths of each member and helping each member to overcome his weaknesses, instead of idealizing some family members and tearing others down.

• Teaching family members the skills needed to overcome failure and to resolve conflict.

Above all, don't give up hope. Just as other issues we have discussed can be resolved, so, too, can this one. But it will take learning certain tasks and renewing your focus on healthy ways to deal with badness. We learn poor ways of dealing with imperfections in a dysfunctional family; the only way to learn to deal with them effectively is in a functional one.

Jesus hinted at this truth when He asked a rhetorical question in reply to the news that His mother and brothers were seeking to speak to Him. "Who is My mother and who are My brothers?" Those who "[do] the will of My Father who is in heaven" (Matthew 12:48–50). We have to find new relationships in the body of Christ that will help us resolve the dysfunctional areas in our lives.

David said it this way: "My eyes shall be on the faithful of the land, that they may dwell with me; He who walks in a blameless way is the one who will minister to me" (Psalm 101:6). David chose his company, or spiritual "family," carefully. So should we.

In the same way, if you need to reform your attitudes regarding badness, failure, or imperfection, it is imperative that you find a support group, safe friend, or counselor. Then you need to put into practice the following steps:

1. Start working on counteracting your belief that perfection is a possibility and/or a demand. It may seem self-evident, but you need also to look at the ways you consciously or unconsciously expect perfection. Ask others to help you. That is real humility—confessing your proud self instead of perpetuating the false humility of denying strengths (James 4:6, 10).

2. List your strengths and weaknesses as honestly as you can, and become comfortable with the existence of those strengths and weaknesses. Until you fully appreciate that you are composed of the good and the bad, and accept that fact, growth will be difficult (Psalm 139:23–24). Get help from your group.

3. List the strengths and weaknesses of those you love. It will be helpful to see them as real people and accept the whole package (Ephesians

4:32). Not judging others is part of learning self-acceptance. That way, the imperfections of others will not creep up and surprise you, even though you have seen them hundreds of times before. If we tend to deny things, it doesn't matter how many times we have seen an imperfection. It always seems like the first, and our reaction reflects our surprise: "How could you have . . . ?" The fact is, we should have expected the imperfection; that is that familiar person's particular weakness. We can never become truly forgiving until we are comfortable with confronting the reality of others' imperfections (Luke 17:3–4).

4. Begin to talk more openly about your negative feelings, and become more accepting of those feelings in others. That will help you get rid of the "all good," way of looking at the world. It will also build intimacy with others, which in turn will lessen your fear of their imperfections. Growth produces growth. Be real (Ephesians 4:25).

5. Work diligently on joining or establishing a support group that will encourage the approach to truth and grace described in this chapter. When it comes to confessing your weaknesses and pains, stay away from perfectionists. They will only judge you and demand more perfection. Align yourself with people who understand the grace of God and practice it (Psalm 101:6–7).

6. Put a serious value on working through conflict with others and re-solving it. That will help you greatly in learning to deal with badness. As you begin to work through conflicts, you will be reinforcing in your own mind the truth that badness does not have to destroy relationships but can actually enhance them (Luke 17:3–4; Proverbs 19:25).

7. Look at whatever area in which you are afraid to risk because of fear of failure or badness. Realize that this fear is a denial of the grace of God and of His willingness to let you fail in order to grow. Begin to step out, and get support from Him and others to learn new ways and skills (Mat-thew 25:24–28).

8. Research causes, and understand them. We repeat generational patterns if we do not acknowledge and repent of them. Left untreated, troubled traditions of the past will bind our future, and the future of our children. Look at the history of dysfunction in the area of facing badness in your family and turn from it.

These steps will start you on the path of overcoming the family dysfunction over imperfections you grew up with. It is liberating to discover that you do not need to be perfect and that you have the freedom to grow and gain support in those areas you might still be failing in.

But remember, as with the other developmental needs, you were made for a family. Even though you came from a dysfunctional one, God wants you to be a part of a functional one now, and you cannot grow apart from that sort of support. Work on getting into a safe setting, and then try the things we have been talking about in this book. Millions of adults recovering from a painful past will testify that they really work.

Questions for Reflection

1. How is the quest for the "ideal me" affecting me and the way I spend my resources (time, energy, money, and so on)?

2. What do I see as the root of the problem?

3. What do I need to change to turn it around?

4. How will I do that?

5. Who will I enlist to help me?

6. When will I do the things I've just listed?

10

Learning to Achieve Adulthood

Henry Cloud

PHIL ENTERED his boss's office with an awful feeling in the pit of his stomach. He didn't know why, since he had been through performance reviews many times before. Rationally, he understood that his boss liked him, but he nevertheless felt afraid.

Among other runaway thoughts, he found himself imagining ways his performance might not be good enough or reasons his boss might disapprove of him personally. The inner turmoil was almost unbearable, yet no matter how he tried to get rid of those feelings, he couldn't. He had tried memorizing Bible verses on fear during the preceding week, but even that didn't seem to help.

Phil got more discouraged as he thought of other situations where similar feelings overtook him. When he went to the elder board meetings at church, he would almost break out in a sweat. He would sit at the table and have all sorts of good ideas, but he was afraid to speak up, fearing someone might disagree or think his ideas were stupid.

As he sat in the board meetings, he would look at the individual members and try to figure out why they seemed so powerful to him, but it made no sense. He was as accomplished as they, at least on the outside, and he should have felt confident about being there. But inside, his feelings of inferiority persisted. He had a recognizable fear that he was "one-down" to the rest of the men. Secretly, he was afraid they might find out.

The same fears would overtake him in social situations as well. When he played golf with his buddies, he would start to think that they were in some way better than he. Some of his friends would occasionally express strong opinions with which he disagreed, but he found himself afraid to express that disagreement. He'd just nod and go along with them, which left him at times feeling ashamed, even wimpy. He just didn't feel like a man around other men. He felt more like a little boy.

If you can identify with Phil, then you know what it is to feel like a "little person in a big person's world." The scenario Phil experienced is predictable for people who grew up in dysfunctional families, even for outwardly successful adults. In a word, they haven't grown up.

God has outlined a system for development, one we have been exploring in these last few chapters. In chapter 7, we looked at how to attach to (bond with) others; in chapter 8, we learned how to be a separate person (set boundaries); and in chapter 9, we learned how to deal with issues of goodness/badness in ourselves and others. In this chapter we are going to look at the next critical link in the chain of recovery: becoming an equal with other adults. I call it "achieving adulthood."

THE PATH

Normal development is a process. In a home, authority is vested in the parents. They are the authorities, the experts in living. Children naturally look to their parents for teaching in all areas of living, from finding food to driving a car. It is a long and painful process, but when it is over, a young adult should feel reasonably comfortable assuming an adult role and exercising authority over his or her life. He should also have reached the point where he feels equal to other adults as siblings under God (Matthew 23:8–10).

There are advantages to assuming an adult position in life. A fully adult person comes out from under a "one-down" position in relation to other adults. He can think and reason for himself. He can choose what to believe and what values to adopt. He can decide which job or career he likes or is best suited for.

As he matures sexually, he can choose appropriate sexual expressions and a mate. He can pursue, develop, practice, and hone his talents. He can establish mutual friendships with other adults, and he can experience the joy of establishing a community of his choice that reflects his preferences. He can choose hobbies and vacations that are to his own liking.

Adulthood is the phase in life characterized by independence of choice and expression. Paul gives us insight into this important developmental passage when he describes the bondage of childhood as compared to human adulthood and becoming a child of God: "As long as the heir is a child, he does not differ at all from a slave although he is owner of everything, but he is under guardians and managers until the date set by the father. So also we, while we were children, were in bondage under the elemental things of the world" (Galatians 4:1–3).

A child is not free. He or she is under the authority or expertise of parents and is, in a real sense, practicing for adulthood. But when the child becomes an adult, he can truly "own" his own life and be his own boss. Ultimately, that is what gives him the freedom to surrender to the authority of God. An adult is the master of whom he will serve, because he decides things for himself.

Compare this freedom to the feeling of being under someone else's rule. You must gain "permission" to have an opinion, make choices, hold beliefs, choose your church—and on and on. It is not a pretty picture, but it is the world in which many often live.

PROBLEMS

It would be nice if everyone grew up in a family that allowed for the kind of development I have just described, a family that supported one's effort toward growth. But not everyone does. Some people grow up in dysfunctional families that do the opposite: They keep the children always in a childish position and send them out into adulthood still feeling "one-down" to other adults. That sort of treatment is a foundation for failure to achieve equality with the adult world.

Let's look at some of the symptoms of feeling "one-down" to other adults:

Extreme Need for Approval

When an adult constantly needs the approval of other adults, it usually means he is stuck in some childish stage of development. He is always looking up to the people around him as though they were parents who held judicial power to certify him as acceptable. But no matter what level of approval he attains, it never is enough. As soon as one person approves of something he does, he feels a need to gain additional approval from someone else. His appetite for approval is insatiable. In one sense it is similar to drug addiction, for the individual caught up in the syndrome is on a merry-go-round of misery that no amount of approval can relieve.

Extreme Fear of Disapproval

An extreme thirst for approval is the motivator of the one-down person's performance. The Bible teaches that we are to be motivated by the grace and acceptance of God and others, and the fear and reverence of God alone. But if we feel we are constantly one-down to all the parent figures around us, then we will constantly fear their disapproval and condemnation. That pattern will yield paralysis life-wide and stunt growth.

Constant and Unrelenting Anxiety

The one-down person experiences constant and unrelenting anxiety. This symptom is not surprising when one considers that the person living in the one-down position sees himself as always subject to criticism and disapproval. That in turn means that, from the one-down person's perspective, every other adult has the power to judge him unacceptable. What a scary way to live!

Avoidance of Risk and Fear of Failure

If we feel one-down to others, we will avoid taking the risks necessary for growth. We can only learn by taking risks and practicing (Matthew 25:26–27; Hebrews 5:13–14), and Jesus commands us to use our talents. But if we are afraid of the opinions and criticisms of others, we have given them parental power and have to avoid their judgment at all costs. Judgment would be too much for us to bear.

Superiority Feelings

If we are stuck in a one-down position in relation to other adults, instead of feeling like equal siblings under God with differing talents (Romans 12:3–8), we will always be comparing ourselves with others to see if we measure up. Invariably this system fails to give us the confidence we need, and we end up feeling inferior to our imagined picture of perfection in others.

On the other hand, if we are particularly aggressive, we may have a tendency to look at others as inferior and try to become a parental authority over them, constantly judging and criticizing. Neither extreme is what God has in mind for maturity.

Extreme Feelings of Competition

Some try to overcome the feeling of being one-down by constantly competing with others. Their goal is to overcome everyone and end up king of the hill. They may win the battle, but they will lose the war, for all their relationships are characterized by power struggles. People don't feel close to them and maintain a distance because they don't trust them.

Powerlessness

Children are by nature "under" the power of adults. That's okay for a child, but as developmental processes take over, this attitude needs to be shed. If a person fails to get rid of it as he grows older, as an adult he will tend to resist expressing assertiveness with other adults. He will be passive in relationships and conflicts and often will feel like a victim in relation to his peers. He will have little sense of direction in his life.

What's more, it will likely be difficult for him to be assertive against evil, even though the Bible commands us to take that position. A verse such as 2 Timothy 1:7 will be emotionally mystifying to him: "For God has not given us a spirit of timidity, but of power and love and discipline." He will truly be handicapped.

"Different Is Wrong" Thinking

Adults naturally differ on many things, such as opinions, tastes, and thoughts. People who still think of themselves in the childish position believe their

thoughts, opinions, and tastes are subject to being judged by the parent figures around them. If their opinions differ from those parent figures, they
automatically see themselves as "wrong." They fear going to the "wrong"
church, wearing the "wrong" clothes, practicing the "wrong" hobbies, and
so on. They experience little sense of freedom to choose their lifestyle and
are subject to a lot of rules. They experience drabness and bondage as they
deny their true selves in the name of this type of thinking.

Rules-dominated Thinking

People who think of themselves as children do not experience the freedom to be governed by principles. Jesus was slow to give rules about anything, but He gave a great many principles. He even provided a principle
to govern all other rules: "Love the Lord your God with all your heart, and
. . . love your neighbor as yourself" (Matthew 22:37–39).

Paul says the same thing in many places, observing that we as children
of God have been freed from parental-type rules (Colossians 2:20–23). He
says that we should not subject ourselves to such rules, for they reduce us
to legalism and take away the freedom that a child of God who is led by
the Spirit should have. But of course if one is afraid of parental or legalistic
disapproval, rules will dominate one's thinking.

Impulsiveness

A child is kept in check by parental structures, or what the Bible speaks of
as the law. But the problem with the law is that it actually has the effect of
leading to greater lawlessness. It produces more rather than less desire,
more rather than fewer sinful impulses (Romans 5:20; 7:5). The person
under the parental commandment of the condemnation of the law ends
up sinning more. He is subject to powerful, almost compulsive behaviors
such as overspending ("I just couldn't help myself"), overeating, and the
like. He feels the "should" of the law and rebels against it. This is the sin-
guilt cycle we identified in chapter 9.

Hatred of Authority

Many who have been crushed by strict authority figures during childhood have not been able personally to identify with the expertise of adulthood. Being an adult means having a certain amount of expertise; you aren't perfect, but you certainly have adult-level talents and strengths. Instead of acquiring this attitude as they grow up, some resent all authority and rebel against it, always trying to find freedom through rebellion.

The problem is that the rebellious child is just as controlled by the parent (even as an adult child) as the compliant child is, only in another direction. The rebellious child may look at first glance as though he is not being controlled by authority, but in reality he is, since his every action is ruled by his reaction to that authority. Rebellion and hatred of authority is a childlike stance, in that one vests all power in authority figures.

Depression

It should be clear by now why this is a depressing way to live. If one constantly feels inferior, guilty, and put down, it is difficult to be happy. Feeling one-down naturally brings with it a good deal of unresolved hurt and anger, which in turn sets a person up for depression in adulthood.

Passive-aggressive Behavior

Passive-aggressive behavior is asserting one's will in an indirect way. Instead of being honest about our aggressive urges, we cloak them in actions that are superficially neutral. We are conveniently late to an appointment with a person with whom we're upset. Perhaps we resent our supervisor on the job, so we struggle with procrastination, never seeming to get to the tasks at hand. Or we might exert an overabundant amount of control in relationships.

Passive-aggressive behavior is a frequent symptom resulting from feeling one-down. The loss of power felt in the one-down position leads to covert attempts at restoration to power through resistance. We see this in the parable of the two sons whose father asked them to work in the vineyard (Matthew 21:28–31). The second son passively obeyed on the outside but resisted on the inside. In the end, he "did not go" (v. 30). He had not yet reached the place where he could openly say no to his parent. But the first brother had reached such a point. His more healthy pattern of saying what he really felt resulted in his being able to change his mind and actually do the work, whereas the second son was stuck in passive resistance and probably resentment.

Person Worship

When someone is still looking at other people as parent figures, he tends to idealize them inappropriately. He will follow them as though they were mini-gods and forget who the real God is. He has failed to make the transition from being under man (his parents) to being under God, as instructed in Matthew 23:8–10: "But do not be called Rabbi; for One is your Teacher, and you are all brothers. Do not call anyone on earth your father; for One is your Father, He who is in Heaven. Do not be called leaders; for One is your Leader, that is, Christ."

Some people caught in this syndrome may worship a pastor or other spiritual leader instead of God, in the name of honoring their leaders. In reality, the practice is a modern-day form of idolatry.

HOW DOES IT HAPPEN?

If it is God's plan for us all to grow up into functioning adults, what goes wrong in a family to prevent that? Let's explore some of the patterns that keep people from achieving adulthood:

Lack of Proper Development in Previous Stages

We've already established that there are stages to normal development, and there are prerequisites that must be fulfilled before a new level of maturity can be approached.

Take the bonding discussed in chapter 7. If a child does not know how to attach emotionally to others, he cannot form the peer support groups that allow him to separate from his family at the age-appropriate level and thus achieve adulthood.

It is important in adolescence for a teen to develop deep attachments to friends and other people outside his home in order to prepare for leaving home. If a teenager does not have skills to form these close and supportive relationships, leaving home and becoming an adult will be impossible for him. He will be like a jet airplane without fuel. He can't fly to new destinations. Appropriate relationships provide the resources for growth through the entire process, and this stage is no different.

Boundaries (chapter 8) are important elements of adulthood, for they teach us a basic sense of responsibility and ownership of our lives. We need to be able to be separate people and become our own people apart from others, thus having our own identity. Boundaries are the cornerstone of this identity formation. Without them, it is impossible to become an adult.

Boundaries define what we think, feel, want, do, choose, and value. The ability to stake out positions in these areas is part of the transition to adulthood and must be well developed if an individual is to keep on moving toward adulthood. If he does not have this capacity, he will not come out from under a one-down opinion of himself, for he will not be able to distinguish his thoughts and feelings from someone else's. He will not be able to overcome parental disapproval of his feelings (and therefore "own" them as an adult) if he is not separate enough from his parents even to know what his own feelings are.

Well-established boundaries provide a sense of limits. If someone is unable to set limits on another's abuse, he is too frightened to go out into the world as an adult. He is still assuming he is to remain forever a child, protected by parent figures from "all the mean people in the world." We need to be able to have good limits to stand as adults.

We need also to be able to set limits on our own behavior and have ample self-control. Having a good sense of boundaries will do this for us, and well-developed self-control is a prerequisite for achieving adulthood. When people lack self-control, they are likely to subject themselves to parent figures to keep themselves in check. That is an ineffective strategy long-term, but it is usually one of the first-line attempts an impulsive person will make as a means of staying in control.

Similarly, persons with this bent will often gravitate toward rigid, legalistic churches and/or dominant spiritual leaders who will "whip them into shape" and "keep them in line." They know they lack self-control and are seeking external vehicles to provide it. But God's ideal is for a person to develop internal self-control as he submits to and is guided by the Holy

Spirit. Self-control is specifically listed in Galatians 5:22–25 as one of the nine elements of the fruit of the Spirit.

With regard to the good/bad struggle discussed in chapter 9, we must be able to handle failure in order to assume adulthood. The extreme need for idealism and perfection in all things is childish. Adults must be able to shift into reality. The real world is imperfect. We must be able to deal with imperfections in ourselves, in others, and in the world around us. People who demand perfection of themselves and others are unable to deal effectively with reality because reality is not perfect. To become the best adults we can be requires the ability to learn, and perfectionists learn very little while demanding a lot.

Authoritarianism

The Bible teaches that parents are to be authorities in the home who "train up a child in the way he should go" (Proverbs 22:6; see also Deuteronomy 6:6–9). The goal is for parents to impart God's ways to the children and get them ready for independence. Developing such independence in a child will require the parent gradually to shift power from himself to the maturing child.

The principle of exercising authority through empowering subjects is seen in many places in the Bible. God the Father gave Jesus all authority and power to accomplish the goals He wanted Jesus to accomplish (Matthew 28:18). When God made Adam, He empowered him by giving him important responsibilities. Adam was to be responsible for the whole earth, to rule and subdue it (Genesis 1:28). There was a real delegation of power from God to Adam.

The earthly family is to be the same way. The parents, as authority figures, are to teach the children how to gain expertise in living and then to become authorities over their own lives. Parents build this expertise in their children through gradually giving over responsibilities to them.

There is a difference between an *authoritative* style of parenting and an *authoritarian* one. In the authoritarian home we do not see a biblical view of authority. The authority figure is dogmatic (dominated by black-and-white thinking), rigid, domineering, and controlling. These characteristics of his behavior keep his children powerless, prohibit learning, and stunt meaningful growth.

In contrast, when a maturing child is learning to deal with, for example, money, the wise (authoritative) parent will allow the child to exercise an appropriate degree of authority over his or her own "assets." Even when the child is anticipating what the parent feels is a dumb buy, the smart parent offers counsel only and lets the child live with the consequences of his purchase decision. Perhaps the child impulsively spends money on inconsequential things and then later lacks the funds to buy something much more important to him; the next time around, saving (self-control) will be more important personally to the child. An important lesson has been learned through the parent's staying out of the process, apart from giving advice. Learning experiences of this kind are the ones that form solid stepping-stones to adulthood.

Authoritarian parenting has been linked in research to many behavioral problems and all sorts of immaturity in children. The New Testament warns the father to avoid provoking his children to anger, causing them to lose heart (Ephesians 6:4; Colossians 3:21). The authoritarian ruling style does not empower the child. Rather, it keeps the child powerless, stifling his maturity and setting the stage for later episodes of aggressive rebellion or for a passive death of the spirit. In contrast to this authoritarian style, the authoritative parenting style positions the parent as an expert in living who passes his expertise on to his children, preparing them for adulthood, and requiring adult self-control from them.

Lack of Practice

Hebrews 5:14 tells us that we mature as we practice. That means families must provide the freedom to fail. Homes that are critical of failure do not produce learning in the child, yet achieving adulthood is practically impossible without learning through failure. Children growing up in a hypercritical atmosphere tend to avoid risk-taking for fear of the consequences.

One young adult told me that as a ten-year-old boy he built a tree house he was very proud of, but his father came home and chewed him out because the angles in the roof weren't "architecturally correct." Every time he tried something new, his father berated him over the particular way he did not do it perfectly. Eventually, he gave up trying. As an adult he was horribly afraid of trying to learn new skills on the job or in his personal life because the threat of failure was too great.

Parenting that does not allow for mistakes sets up a fear dynamic in the child that inhibits learning, for it is difficult to learn when one is dominated by fear. What a contrast to our heavenly Father, who "knows our frame" (Psalm 103:14) and is "slow to anger" (Psalm 103:8). As parents we ought to follow His practice, patiently watching our children grow toward adulthood.

Lack of Resources

Some parents do not look for emerging talents in their children and fail to provide them with the resources they need to develop their talents. God has given everyone talents and abilities, and parents need to provide their children with the resources for developing them.

There are parents who withhold resources even when they are available. Being too poor to provide resources is one thing, but withholding support that is possible financially is quite another. What is involved here are specific kinds of refusals: not allowing a child to attend workshops, clubs, or join sports teams, refusing to buy necessary sports equipment, refusing to help with the purchase of costumes for dramatic productions at school, and so on. In the healthy family, if a child shows some ability, the parent tries to provide the setting and tools needed to develop that skill.

Invariably the child will do some shopping around to find his niche or area of expertise and interest. Too many parents give up at this stage. When a child wants to try a new skill, they say, "No, I won't allow you to play baseball. Remember when you were going to learn to ski? I sent you on that church trip and spent all that money, and you haven't been skiing since." Now I'm not advocating reckless spending of money. Instead, I'm encouraging a bit of freedom for kids trying to find their niche. That will normally involve some false starts. That's okay. No one knows what he is going to wind up liking without trying it out first.

On the other hand, I'm not advocating indulgence. If a child wants to learn horseback riding, the parent need not rush out and buy a ranch. There needs to be a balance between providing resources where they are available, but providing them appropriately for the level of the child (the parents' task), and the exercise of responsibility by the child for that same level. When the child is faithful here, that could lead to future opportunities.

Permissiveness

The extreme opposite of the authoritarian parent is the overly permissive parent who establishes insufficient authority in the home and provides little in the way of limits. Such a parent does not provide an adequate structure for the child to learn right from wrong or to learn to be an authority as an adult later in life (Proverbs 19:18). There is nothing wrong with parents being the boss. Parental authority is necessary, for parents really do know more about life. What's more, God desires it. But He does not advocate dictatorship.

The problem comes with the extremes of too authoritarian or too permissive a style. The result is either lawlessness (in the latter case) or identity confusion (in the former). We need a balance of structure and limits for a secure sense of who we are.

Inconsistency

The inconsistent style vacillates between authoritarianism and permissiveness. It sets up a split in the child between impulsiveness that knows no limits and guilt that knows only limits.

Many parents are in conflict over their own sense of authority. As a result, they act out in both directions with the child. When parents vacillate between permissiveness and authoritarianism, the child never develops a consistent authority structure within himself. He is either impulsive or guilty, as erratic as the home structure. The result is chaos, both in the family and within each personality.

Lack of Respect for Personal Differences

In the authoritarian home, compliance is the norm. But in reality, people are different from one another. They have different tastes, opinions, and talents, to name but a few. In some homes this difference among individuals is punished, unnoticed, or in some way devalued. That keeps the child from developing an adult identity.

The child in such a home fears differing from his parents' choices. He may not want to be a professional like Dad; he may not want to be a missionary like Grandfather; he may not like sports but instead prefers music. There may be many differences he will want to express. But he knows that expressing those differences will not be accepted in his home. Children like this sometimes have to become "black sheep" in order to avoid conformity and fusion with others. Their differences need to be accepted and brought to maturity.

Imbalance of Love and Limits

Developing authority over one's adult life comes from an internalization of the style of parents who balanced love and limits. As children observe their parents, they take their balance into their own souls. Parents who balance love and limits have children who are independent, outgoing, and social.

On the other hand, when there is an imbalance of love and limits, problematic combinations develop. A home atmosphere might be loving (good) but controlling (bad); or loving (good) but permissive (bad); or controlling (bad) and unloving (bad again). All of these confusing parenting combinations produce authority problems in children.

The Bible tells us that there should be standards and limits in a home but also grace and love. This combination reflects God's very nature, which is sometimes described as being composed of justice (limits) and mercy (love). Whenever there is an imbalance of justice or mercy, we have left out one side of the nature of God, and all will suffer from that imbalance.

Denial of Sexuality

Achieving adulthood includes learning about our God-given sexuality. Homes that exclude sexuality from normal existence prohibit development into healthy adulthood. Here, as elsewhere, balance is important. Homes that repress any sexual aspects of the personality do not allow the child to grow into adult sexuality, whereas permissive homes sometimes overwhelm a child with sexual impulses. Some homes are so Victorian that even mentioning sex is a mortal sin, whereas others have virtually no sense of decency or modesty.

Sexuality must be balanced in the home for a little person to incorporate that aspect of his or her personhood into existence and thus become a "big person." Homes that avoid or repress sexuality can cause teens to fear their sexuality and thus avoid adulthood, or even act it out prematurely. Permissive homes, on the other hand, force children into adulthood much too early, causing equally grievous problems.

Sexuality needs to be talked about and affirmed in its rightful place, given a high value, and placed within biblically appropriate boundaries. That will allow the child to grow up in touch with his sexuality and free of shame and guilt, while at the same time having self-control.

Convictions of the Heart That Prevent Achieving Adulthood

Let's look now at some of the attitudes of the heart that can stifle our move to adulthood. Consider whether any apply to you or to your upbringing. Sometimes these distortions, as listed in an absolute form, appear extreme or ridiculous, but many of these attitudes can creep into our thinking in lesser degrees and still cause problems in achieving adulthood.

Distortions about God:
- God is dogmatic about everything and does not like me to question things; such questions represent a lack of faith.
- God is a rigid parent who will crush me if I disagree with Him.
- God wants me to be a clone of my spiritual leaders and authority figures and to do everything their way.
- God does not allow me freedom in the grey areas of Christian conduct, such as entertainment options; in fact, I doubt whether there even are grey areas in God's view.
- God will punish me when I try to learn new things and don't execute them perfectly.
- God does not like me to have my own opinions; having my own opinions would be rebellion.

Distortions about others:
- People are critical and disapproving of my actions and thoughts.
- People won't allow me to fail and thus learn to do better.
- Others will hate me if I disagree with them.
- Others will like me better if I am compliant to their wishes, demands, and plans.
- Others never fail like I always seem to be doing; they seem to know everything.
- My leaders are perfect; they have no weaknesses; their beliefs are better than mine; they know what I should do better than I do; they are always right.

Distortions about ourselves:
- I am worthless if others don't approve of me.
- I should never have tried that; I really messed it up; I am a miserable failure.
- I have no right to my opinions; they are usually wrong anyway.
- My beliefs are the only right ones.
- I know what is best for him or her.
- I should always do what I am told.
- My sexual feelings are bad.
- I shouldn't feel angry / disappointed / sad / lonely (and so on).
- I will never measure up to him or her.

NEW ATTITUDES AND ACTIVITIES THAT YIELD GROWTH

In order for us to achieve adulthood and grow past a dysfunctional background, we must challenge old ways and practices. That will require new skills.

Before we look at those skills, though, let us emphasize that there is no solid, long-term growth apart from the body of Christ. You must get into supportive, Christian relationships that encourage your movement into adulthood. That is the way it should have happened the first time around. You were designed to begin to develop relationships outside the home when you were still a teenager that would help you join the family of adult brothers and sisters as a peer. It is just as crucial now for you to do so.

Let's look at some of those skills:

1. *Confess to God and to others your need to become an adult* (Matthew 5:3; James 5:16). God and His family (the church) feel okay about your inadequacies in this area; they do not expect you to be all grown up all at once. Find a family of believers who will accept your present state of maturity and encourage you into adulthood by gently pushing you back onto the playing field of life when you skin your knees.

2. *Develop a theology that allows for the concept of practice.* You are about to embark on a road of learning; there is no way for you to know already what you need to learn. Give up the need to be there already, and get onto the practice field. The only the way to gain expertise is through practice.

3. *Find your talents and pursue them.* God has given you certain talents and abilities He wants you to develop. In fact, He will be displeased if you refuse to try to develop and use them (Matthew 25:14–29). He is on your side in this endeavor (Romans 8:31–32).

4. *Become aware of your own opinions and thoughts.* Adults think for themselves. You should listen to counsel from teachers and experts (Proverbs 11:14), but it's okay to develop your own expertise in important areas so that you don't constantly need parent figures to make your decisions for you. This point applies also to husbands and wives, as many times they will turn their respective spouses into "parent figures." Pray for guidance and wisdom (Psalm 32:8). God wants to teach you in many areas, and He will guide you to the information you need. Gather lots of data from the experts, but then identify what you believe. That will keep you from being a groupie or a cult member.

5. *Respectfully disagree with authority figures when you have a different opinion.* This sort of assertiveness is the only way to get into dialogue, which is where we learn. The authority figures we are talking about include God. If you disagree with Him about something, tell Him. Job and David did (Job 10:1–22;

Psalm 22:2). That was the beginning of dialogue and learning for them. This capacity for dialogue needs to appear in a marriage, too; wives and husbands need to learn how to disagree with one another respectfully when their opinions differ. In terms of people in general, you may be surprised that even the authorities can learn something sometimes and change their position.

6. *Dethrone people whom you may have put on pedestals* (1 John 5:21). If you have set anyone up as perfect, you have set him up as an idol. Try to see him (or her) more realistically and as a brother or sister instead of a parent. Your goal is to achieve brotherhood with men and establish the Fatherhood of God (Matthew 23:8–9). Here again, wives who enthrone their husbands (or husbands who enthrone their wives) need to think through what it means for them as adults to place someone in such a position.

7. *Submit freely to those in roles of authority over you.* Submission proves our freedom; rebellion against authority proves our childish state. The equality-minded adult is able to submit to a God-ordained role in the same way he submits to God and does not feel as though he is somehow giving in (Romans 13:1). Submission is not putting someone on a pedestal. The process of finding the right balance is complicated, as you both disagree and submit. There will be some trial and error at first. And once a balance is struck it shouldn't be considered sacred. Seasons of life change, and individuals change; so, too, may the balance that "feels right" vary later on.

8. *Treat others as equals.* Do not parent them; yet do not allow yourself to be controlled or judged by them either. To do the latter is to put yourself or them under the law. In the free / grey areas, make up your own mind and allow others to do so also (Romans 14:22; Colossians 2:16–19). Here again, wives and husbands need to see their spouses as equals and not as parents or as children.

9. *Give up your rigid thinking and don't succumb to the black-and-white thinking of others.* Appreciate the things that we cannot know for sure (Romans 11:33–36). That is to allow God to be God and us to be human. Give up the need to have certainty and rules for everything. Worship God, not rules.

10. *Deal with sexuality.* If you are afraid of your sexual feelings, get in a setting where it is safe to talk about them, and accept them without shame. Remember, shame is a product of the fall (Genesis 3:10). Marriage is a wonderful opportunity often ignored by Christian couples to talk about sexual feelings. Sexuality is something you talk about in marriage, not just something you do. Sexuality is good when it is practiced under God's guidelines; He made it.

11. *Take responsibility for your life.* When you were a child, you were under the rule of stewards and managers, typically parents (Galatians 4:1–3). But as an adult, you are no longer under their responsibility. You are now the steward of your life. This holds true for married people as well as for singles. Marriage is a partnership, a yoking of two walking along together, but each of the partners must assume responsibility for his own life. In fact, it is a misunderstanding on this very point that leads to the enabling behavior exhibited by spouses married to persons caught up in compulsive disease. Accept responsibility for enabling, and require responsibility from the spouse.

12. *Look at every adult around you as an equal.* These adults—and they include your spouse—may have very different talents and experiences, but you are equal to them in terms of worth. Learn to cherish your differences instead of being judged by them or by being proud (Romans 12:3–8).

13. *Realize where you disagree with your parents.* The Bible tells us that we are to examine our actions and avoid blindly doing things according to the "tradition of the elders" instead of God's ways (Matthew 15:1–3). Distinguish your plans and views from those of your parents.

14. *Pursue your dreams.* Share your dreams with God, and allow Him to shape them (Proverbs 16:3). Then go for it!

Questions for Reflection

1. In what ways do I feel I am one-down to others? In what areas do I most keenly feel this?

2. What has caused such feelings?

3. What attitudes do I need to change to gain equality with other adults?

4. How do I still have my parents (or other authority figures) on a pedestal? How can I get them off the pedestal?

5. With which of their thoughts do I disagree?

6. What about my thoughts and opinions? Do I value them adequately? If not, how can I improve in this area?

7. Who am I inappropriately allowing to parent me? How will I stop?

8. Where will I go for mutual support? When?

11

Facing Life's "Unfair Assignments"

Dave Carder

JULIE (see Introduction) put her journal on her lap and sighed during a review of her spiritual and emotional odyssey of the previous eighteen months. She was gradually learning to bond with her children and her second husband. She was still experiencing the anxiety that accompanies change. It seemed as though she always felt vulnerable; she wanted so badly to start feeling normal. She wanted the normal experience of feeling close to those she loved without it feeling so scary. Everything seemed like such hard work. Why did God make relationships so difficult, anyway? Oh well, she thought, at least she was making progress.

Julie was also learning to say yes and no more appropriately. She was feeling more in control of herself and her personal environment. For that she was glad. However, she had to admit that at times even that area appeared to be going backward. Why did everything seem to take so much time?

She could admit to herself now (and even, on occasion, to others) that she had many good qualities. When she failed, she found herself picking up the pieces more quickly and getting back on track sooner than she ever had before. She remembered the days when failure led to one kind of out-of-control eating binge after another. Now, she was thankful, all that seemed far away.

She also was feeling quite pleased about her newfound ability to stand up to authority figures such as her parents or her boss. She would never forget the years she cowered in the presence of those more powerful than she and then later, after their abuse, acted out her rage at them with flagrant abandon.

Entire months, entire years, were still missing from her memory. Some memories were probably gone forever, due to the drugs and alcohol she had consumed during those periods. Other memories she would just as soon not think about anyway, though at times they seemed right on the verge of returning, much like an unwanted relative. There had been such inner turmoil during those periods that she couldn't sleep and food had no taste. Neither sleep nor food could satisfy even temporarily, as it used to. She had felt so many panic feelings during those episodes that she'd often worried whether she would either fall apart or fly into uncontrollable rage.

As Julie continued to reflect on the transition that had occurred in her life, she recalled talking with her counselor about her "Gethsemane" experience as Julie called it. She could feel this process at work. The focus of her recovery was shifting from what she could rebuild to what she had to accept as unchangeable.

It seemed so unfair—and it *was*. If a loving God created children and put them in families, why had He given Julie to such angry parents? She still couldn't understand that. She was so fragile, and they had been so brutal. It didn't make sense.

Jesus called the little children to Him when He taught, yet as a child Julie had felt abandoned by Jesus. She could feel the pain welling up within her as she allowed herself to think about the reality of her experience. On many occasions she had curled up on the sofa in a fetal curl, convulsed by uncontrollable sobs. Her pillow was frequently soaked with tears.

In retrospect, Julie realized that through it all Jesus really had been there with her. His presence in her pain had been her only resource. He was as real as her desperation required. At times she felt Him sitting on the bed beside her. Other times He had seemed simply to hold her hand and say, "I know."

GETHSEMANE: JESUS UNDERSTANDS

In many years of ministry to others in recovery and, indeed, in working through my own recovery, I have found it is a supreme comfort to realize that our Savior has been there before us. In addition to feeling massive physical pain as He hung on the cross, Jesus felt excruciating emotional pain. Nowhere is this fact more evident than in the account of Jesus in the garden of Gethsemane (Matthew 26:36–46; Mark 14:32–42; Luke 22:39–46). Julie, whose story we examined at the outset of this book and again in this chapter, is in the midst of a process with numerous parallels to Jesus' experience in the garden.

This fact should encourage us to come boldly to the Lord for help in times of trouble because He understands what it is like to go through suffering (Hebrews 2:14–15; 4:14–16).

Some of the parallels between Jesus' work in the garden and the recovery from a difficult family background are offered here as an encouragement to those in the midst of agony. This teaching does not represent a series of steps or stages that everyone in recovery *must* pass through, nor does it represent the *only* way to "work through" an issue. It is simply an account of Jesus' personal pattern.

By examining the parallels between Jesus' Gethsemane experience and our own recovery, I am in no way implying that Jesus was dysfunctional. He simply did some very healthy things in dealing with His emotions that night in the garden, and we can benefit from His practice. He was fully God and man during His years on earth, and in His humanity we can see health-giving patterns.

You will develop a recovery style that fits you, your personality, and your situation as you pursue your own pilgrimage. It might be somewhat different from the one examined here, but it will probably have many parallels to Jesus' Gethsemane experience of coming to terms with something so painful every cell in your body wants to avoid it. Jesus was able to walk *through*, instead of *around*, His Gethsemane; in studying His experience, we can glean ways of handling our most difficult life assignments.

JESUS WAS VULNERABLE TO PAIN BECAUSE HE LOVED

Jesus was in Gethsemane because He loved us, you and me. If He had not loved us so much, the experience of the cross and the process of preparation in Gethsemane would not have been so painful. He was torn because He fully felt the emotional agony of the experience. Unlike many who struggle or some parents of those who struggle, He didn't practice emotional stifling. He didn't say, as many parents have said, "Suck it up, stop crying, it's going to be all right," or, "Don't be so emotional—just hurry up and make a decision," or, "You can't change it, so just go on and forget it."

The hurt and memories of a child from an alcoholic or dysfunctional family linger and are almost overwhelming because of the love the child has for his parents. Sure, he cannot change the past. Sure, he is a Christian now. But he still wants intensely to change the experience he had. Jesus, the omnipotent Son of God, wanted just as intensely, at the outset, to change His experience: "Everything is possible for you. Take this cup from me" (Mark 14:36 NIV).

Jesus eventually gave His life for the ones He loved; so also the child from a dysfunctional family becomes willing to "give his life" for his family. For a long time Julie bore all her family's pain in order to keep her family together. Out of love she truly sacrificed a large part of herself. Other children might similarly keep quiet about wrongs done to them so as not to hurt a parent or not to injure what they perceive as a very fragile relationship.

JESUS STRUGGLED WITH FEELINGS OF ABANDONMENT

Though the moment of total abandonment would come later at the cross, there in Gethsemane a growing sense of aloneness welled up inside of Jesus. Accompanied perhaps by the feeling that no one really understood what it was like to carry His pain, He felt more and more isolated as He came to grips with its agony. He was consumed with the struggle. He even cut Himself off, to some degree, from His three closest disciples by going a little farther into the garden to pray alone (Matthew 26:39). His other close friends, supposedly there to comfort Him, were sleeping. He felt as though He would explode from the internal pressure. You know how it is if you have ever struggled emotionally: sweat, tears, runny nose. You feel flushed, intensely tight on the inside. Jesus experienced that same distress.

JESUS WENT TO A SPECIAL PLACE TO DO THE "WORK"

When the Last Supper was over and the moment finally came to face the pain, Jesus went to His special place, Gethsemane (Matthew 26:36). He had visited it many times. There, in that familiar place, He had in the past repeatedly experienced a sense of comfort and relief.

Every child in a dysfunctional family has a Gethsemane, a place where she can pour out her heart, a place where she feels understood and from which she leaves with a sense of relief. It might be a hideout in the backyard or an empty lot next door where he can cuddle with the dog. It might be a closet where he can cry for extended periods, alone and unheard. Maybe it is only her bed and a stuffed animal to hug there, but it is a refuge in a painful world. When there are few quality relationships in a child's family of origin, that special place takes preeminence. It becomes the point of attachment where a sense of belonging, a sense of being "at home," warms the little heart. Like Jesus' refuge the night before the cross, that place becomes a Gethsemane.

Going through recovery, you will often come upon a second Gethsemane experience, a transition period that occurs between the phase of learning about what happened to you as a child and the phase of actually having to do something about it. You are at the stage where you must face tough "work," the task of working through difficult personal issues.

When the time has come to work through a painful experience, make sure you have found a new "familiar place" to go. This is where a long-term relationship with the Lord can be very important. Many have been on the run from family, God, and most other relationships. They have cut themselves off from painful experiences, preferring to journey through life emotionally numb and alone. Survival has been their all-consuming goal.

Eventually, though, the pain returns, simply because life is cyclical. Then that new haven becomes important. It will provide a safe place where you can talk, feel listened to while you unload, and from which you can walk away, leaving your burden behind you. That safe place might be a support group.

SIMPLY KNOWING ABOUT THE CROSS DID NOT "FIX" JESUS' FEELINGS

Information is usually helpful and facts are always necessary, but knowledge alone is not sufficient when emotions are involved. Jesus knew He would go to the cross, He even *chose* to go, but He still needed to work through the feelings involved. His intense distress caused him to pray with much agony to His heavenly Father.

Obtaining knowledge about forgiveness and choosing to forgive are not the same as struggling through the feelings of dealing with the unfairness that surround the circumstances requiring forgiveness. It was in Gethsemane that Jesus truly came to grips with the cost of forgiveness. If anyone was capable of "just deciding" to forgive (without processing the emotions), as many well-meaning friends often advise those struggling with forgiveness to do, Jesus certainly was. He could have toughed it out, sucked it up, let it go. But He didn't.

Jesus' Gethsemane experience says to us that feelings are real and valid and need to be worked through. That is one of the purposes of Gethsemane: Jesus wanted to show us how to work through the difficult, unfair, and usually unasked-for assignments in life. The pilgrim walking through a painful family-of-origin recovery process will have to follow his Master's path: right through the middle of the pain. Avoiding such a difficult process is not sufficient. Otherwise Jesus' journey would have led straight from the Last Supper to the cross. Similarly, we can learn from Gethsemane that feelings are not necessarily to be trusted to dictate a course of action. If that were true, Jesus would have never gone to the cross!

JESUS SAID IT BEFORE HE BELIEVED IT

One of the wonderful encouragements of the great struggle in Gethsemane is that Jesus had to pray the same prayer three times (Matthew 26:36–44). Can you imagine that? The Son of God had to repeat Himself! You and I tend to need to pray the same prayers again and again, and even the apostle Paul prayed multiple times about his thorn in the flesh (2 Corinthians 12:8), but we usually do not think that Jesus would ever have to do that.

Why do we think Jesus shouldn't have had to pray over and over? In part because we tend to equate repeating prayers with inefficiency or ineffectiveness, which we consider bad. *One time should do it*, we think, and then we feel guilty when we bring a certain matter up in prayer again. Jesus in Gethsemane shows us that it is okay to struggle.

For those of us who are compulsive about scratching things off our "to do" lists and pronouncing them "done" with an air of satisfaction and accomplishment, this picture of Jesus repeating his prayer is alarming. How many times have you decided to forgive others during times of prayer, got up off your knees, and thought, *I'm glad I'm through with that*, only to have to repeat the process the next day or the next week? Sound familiar? Repeating difficult prayers over a period of time is not only okay, it is downright helpful. And, I might add, it is good to say prayers out loud, too, especially when you are by yourself.

JESUS DID THE WORK IN STAGES

Jesus did His work at Gethsemane in separate distinct periods (three prayer sessions), each ending with a conversation with His support group, the disciples. Here we see that time is important to the process. Jesus worked on the issue at hand with all the time He had, but He did not work on it all of the time. Most of us typically want to cram a childhood of tough experiences into one prayer session or one week of nonstop reading if possible.

But recovery doesn't work that way. It takes time to recover from childhood hurts. Jesus' pattern allowed for intense times of struggle followed by relief. In between normal conversations with His friends He returned to the struggle, as it welled up within.

Recovery work often parallels the original creative work of God in Genesis. Each new day brought progress toward the goal of a perfect and complete environment. But each day was also complete in itself. For example, each day after Day 2 received the same benediction, "It was good," as did Day 6, when the project was complete: "Behold, it was very good" (for these benedictions see Genesis 1:10, 12, 18, 21, 25, 31). In contrast to God's way, many of us would have pronounced only Day 6 "good," because that was when the project was finished. We fail to see each step of the journey as good and impatiently await the final outcome before we can feel any satisfaction about the project.

One of the twelve themes of the A.A. (Alcoholics Anonymous) movement is summarized in the phrase "one day at a time." That is exactly the process God used in creation when He recognized each day as complete in itself, even though the entire project was unfinished. That is also the same process used in sanctification: We will never be perfect in the recovery and growth God brings about in our lives, short of heaven. But the daily progress we make as we walk with Him can be reassuring, if we'll view it that way as we take life day by day, one step at a time.

There is another application of this idea to parenting and recovery: If we as parents would accept the fact that the *product* of our parenting (our children) lies in God's hands, whereas He has only placed the *process* in ours, we would do much better. God wants us to focus on the process, not the outcome. Remember, most of us left home "half-baked," and God has brought us through it all; He will bring your children through it, too.

JESUS STAYED CLOSE TO HIS "SUPPORT GROUP"

At Gethsemane, it was time for the Master to be ministered to. Going into His greatest trial, He wanted His support group close at hand. He'd invested three years with them; they knew Him well. They had been through the good and the bad together. He motioned to the eight where He wanted them to stay and took His three closest friends a little farther on. He wanted to know exactly where everybody was as He prepared to go through His struggle.

One reason Gethsemane experiences are so tough on some people is that the individuals going through them lack a support group. They don't have the multilayered network Jesus established over the last three years of His life on earth.

As the pressure built, Jesus chose to be with friends instead of family in this crisis experience. Many commentators say the disciples let Him down, that His support group failed Him at the moment of their greatest opportunity. Luke (22:46) suggests otherwise, when he reports that when Jesus finds them sleeping, it is a sleep brought about by exhaustion from sorrow. They have grieved to their limit.

Similarly, it is critical for us to remember that recovery can be supported only so far by others. A support group can sustain one through just so much and for only so long. Because the grieving person hurts so badly, he often has impossible expectations of his friends. Jesus did not let this disappointment with his friends deter Him from the task at hand. Back He goes, to work on it some more alone in prayer.

JESUS DID THE HARD WORK HIMSELF—ALONE

Recovery is a personal assignment that only you can tackle. No one else can do it for you. No one else can feel as deeply as you do about the issues affecting you. No pastor, no counselor, no support group can wrap it up for you. They can stand with you for a while, but the hard work you will often do by yourself in the middle of the night without a lot of support, except for the Son of Man who has gone through it before you (Hebrews 2:14–18; 4:14–16).

JESUS RECOGNIZES OUR VULNERABILITY TO TEMPTATION

Jesus in the garden urged His disciples to pray for strength in resisting temptation (Matthew 26:41).

The pain encountered while doing work in recovery is often so intense that we crave relief in any form. We each have our own vulnerabilities, and ways we seek relief, and that need for relief will become almost irresistible as we approach the apex of the pain. For some, relief will take the form of a craving to eat, for others it will be a craving for drink, and for still others it will be the impetus to work ourselves to death or to exercise until we injure ourselves. Whatever your area of vulnerability, be especially alert in times of turmoil.

It is often during times like this that the temptation for illicit sexual activity flourishes. If the spouse is not nurturing to the sufferer, or if an individual is single and dating, this vulnerability to temptation can be intense. He feels a need for someone to care, someone to hold, someone to understand and reassure. What often starts as a simple, caring, platonic relationship can escalate into a flaming infatuation overnight.

Sexual temptation resulting from intense intimacy is one of the dangers of a support group. Many times a simple nod of the head, word of affirmation, or "brotherly hug" is so refreshing to a barren soul that it is misinterpreted as meaning more than was originally intended. But relationships developed in the midst of pain cannot last. The pain won't always be there, and once it diminishes, so does the need for that relationship.

That is exactly why second marriages have higher divorce rates than first marriages. Those relationships are often formed in the midst of one partner's (or both partners') pain, and that temporary need overshadows all other components of a healthy marriage. As was pointed out in chapter 2, this is probably why Isaac and Rebekah had such a tough time. Isaac had never worked through his separation from his mother prior to marrying Rebekah. Instead, he used his marriage to attempt to heal his extended grief over his mother's death.

GETHSEMANE OCCURRED IN MID-LIFE

In a time when the life span was somewhat shorter than it is today, Jesus had reached mid-life by the time of his Gethsemane. During mid-life many of us reach the point where we need to go back before we know we can go on. Our own children have provoked feelings requiring evaluation. Our aging parents remind us that time is running out. There is a growing sense that the clock is working against us.

This is to be expected, because a person's mid-life anticipates some major role reversals. Soon a middle-aged person's aging parents will become like the children, and the children will become like the parents. Often long-buried secrets from the family of origin surface during mid-life. That is one reason we have so much "elder abuse" in the land today. Children who were abused when they were young are growing older, changing roles in relationship to their own parents, and treating those parents exactly how they were once treated as children. Having never been able to talk about the earlier abuse, they now act out their rage against those who practiced it against them. The unresolved issues from the past create an explosive situation.

Even if one's family of origin was not abusive, the original family pattern has a tendency to be repeated when the roles reverse at mid-life. If a parent was absent, the adult child will not want to visit his parents very often. If a parent was controlling, the adult child will respond the same way. If the parent was always irritated, the adult child is often angry beyond what circumstances warrant. The roles of parent and child may change, but the pattern between the parent and child won't unless the adult child works through unresolved issues.

Once one has resolved some of the unfinished business of her family of origin, she is more accepting toward her parents and can even achieve the ultimate sign of recovery: caring for the parents who wounded her while in the midst of her own pain. Though Jesus had no unfinished business to clear up personally, we see Him demonstrating the ideal of caring for aging parents. As He hung from the cross, one of His last statements (John 19:25–27) was directed toward the care of His mother, who was probably a widow by that time.

JESUS DEFERRED THE OPTION OF CONFRONTING HIS ATTACKERS

Gethsemane closes, as does all recovery, with the task of confronting the people who helped to cause the pain. Peter initiated the effort by cutting off a man's ear with his sword. But Jesus, knowing the right action to take at this critical juncture, said in effect, "Now is not the time" (see Matthew 26:45–57; John 18:10–11). Jesus could have blasted that mob in the garden, but instead He chose to defer confrontation until a more appropriate time. At His second coming, Jesus will confront those who hurt Him; His scars will condemn them (Revelation 1:7).

Similarly, in recovery, though confrontation is often helpful it must sometimes be deferred. The timing varies with each case: Sometimes confrontation can occur early, other times late. And, though it is often best to receive some coaching from a Christian confidante about how the confrontation should proceed, the timing of that confrontation is best left up to the individual. He will know when it is time.

Before confrontation, work through the anger and hurt you feel. Otherwise confrontation will become retaliation that leaves you resentful because it brings no relief. Confrontation is different from revenge. That is why the Lord urges, "Never take your own revenge, beloved, but leave room for the wrath of God, for it is written, 'Vengeance is Mine, I will repay,' says the Lord" (Romans 12:19).

Jesus' future confrontation at His second coming invalidates the all-too-common advice given to many who are processing anger against parents or others: "Well, that's water under the bridge. It's in the past. It won't do any good to go back and to confront them. Just leave it alone. What's done is done. You can't change the past." Such advice is usually based on fear of confrontation in general. Confrontation is often viewed wrongly as perpetuating anger, and that view can prevent the individual from experiencing a healthy resolution to the recovery process. Jesus will one day confront those who have wronged Him in His past, and it is okay for you, as His child, to do the same.

Sometimes the individuals who contributed to the pain are no longer living. That does not erase the need for accomplishing confrontation and forgiveness. Many have found it helpful to write a letter to their deceased parent(s), as seen and experienced through their eyes as children. They write down all of the feelings they wanted to say "at the time" but could not. So it is important for the recovering adult, after writing his "child's letter," to read it out loud now, perhaps even reading it before a photograph of the deceased.

Often writing the letter provides enough relief, but you may find it necessary to visit the gravesite and actually read the letter aloud, as if directly to the parents who are now gone. This exercise is simply for your sake. The goal is to help you verbalize what has been left unspoken for so long.

Confrontation never changes what has been done in the past, but it can stop the repetition of the pattern. It also allows the perpetrator an opportunity to gain some sense of relief from the guilt he feels, *if he is able verbally to acknowledge his wrongdoing.* Finally, the injured one can feel affirmed and invested with newfound dignity. He has managed to stand up against his attacker (before whom he formerly cowered emotionally). The self-respect he thus gains will speed the recovery process.

JULIE, JESUS, AND YOU: LETTING GO

During the recovery process, Julie received word from her parents that her father had become ill. Since returning home required a substantial drive and since she hadn't been back in several years, she decided this might be the time to confront her father about his abuse and her mother about the incident of sexual molestation. She hoped their acknowledgment and brokenness over the experiences would provide additional relief for her and for them.

Unfortunately, that relief for Julie never came. Her dad justified his rage, and her mom denied her behavior. Initially, Julie was devastated, but gradually her depression lifted, and she came to accept that she would have to work on forgiving her parents without an acknowledgment from them that they needed to be forgiven.

This is the pain of the cross, the pain Jesus must have felt as He hung dying for millions of people who would never acknowledge their need for His death. As Julie struggled with forgiveness, she more than once thought in anguish, *Why go through this forgiveness when they don't even want it?* Truly "the fellowship of His sufferings" (Philippians 3:10) is often all that supports anyone going through this struggle.

One final element needs to be addressed: "letting go." To let go of something is the essence of the Serenity Prayer, which has ministered to millions of adults recovering from a troubled childhood, as well as to other sufferers:

> God, grant me the serenity
> to accept the things I cannot change,
> the courage to change the things I can,
> and the wisdom to know the difference.
> Living one day at a time,
> enjoying one moment at a time,
> accepting hardship as a pathway to peace;
> taking, as Jesus did,
> this sinful world as it is,
> not as I would have it,

trusting that You will make all things right
if I surrender to Your will;
so that I may be reasonably happy in this life
and supremely happy with You forever in the next. Amen.
(Reinhold Niebuhr)

Jesus died for those millions who would never care that He did so. Jesus truly let go: He did not force everyone in the world to become a believer. God gives free will to all of His human creation. That is the ultimate letting go. God chose to let the first pair of humans go against Him in the garden of Eden, and He sees fit to let millions continue to do so.

We, too, need to let go of the outcome of the recovery process. We cannot force other people to forgive, to change their minds, to apologize. And, of course, they cannot live their lives over. We cannot make another pay for the past, though we may often wish we could. We can only be responsible for our own responses in the present and for our future choices. In our walk of accountability before the Lord, we need to work through the process of recovery so we can reach the ultimate stage of forgiveness. The bottom line is that there are no excuses for not working through life's unfair assignments.

Recovery from a hurtful family past is never easy, but it is always good. And though it may seem at times to be impossibly difficult, God is there for those who want to do it right, in His strength, in His power, and under His care, guidance, and healing hand.

Questions for Reflection

1. After reading this chapter, how do you feel about:
   - the concept of Gethsemane experiences as a whole?
   - the process you might have to go through?
   - the area of confrontation: how, why, and when?
   - the idea expressed at the chapter's conclusion: that there is no excuse for not addressing forgiveness?

2. Have you ever been through a Gethsemane experience? If so, have you ever told anyone else about that experience? What do you wish had happened differently in your Gethsemane experience?

3. Who is your support group? What kinds of experiences have you had together that make you think those persons would see themselves as a support group for you?

4. To whom do you offer support? For what? How often? What kind? What could you do differently?

5. What responses are you going through in relation to this book? Which chapter or section:
   • has been the most/least helpful? Why or why not?
   • has been the hardest to understand? The easiest?
   • has matched your own experience the best?
   • has been the most unsettling for you?

6. What are some action steps you might take now in relation to what you have read in this book?

Appendix A

ALTHOUGH the following information specifically addresses families in full-time ministry work, the teaching widely applies to all those who serve kingdom interests, including lay people.

HELPING THE HELPERS: DYSFUNCTIONAL FAMILIES IN "THE MINISTRY"
Contributor: *Alice Brawand, MA*

People who enter the ministry are often "people helpers" at heart—which is admirable. But when they carry people-helping to such an extreme that they cannot feel good about themselves unless they are continually doing good for others, even to the point of joylessness and exhaustion, they have fallen into a problematic pattern.

Eventually, a slow resentment will build as they find themselves "manipulated" by unreasonable demands. Unless their own deeper needs are satisfied and unless they learn some of the healthy patterns described in this book, burnout and dropout will almost surely result.

They should be aware of the following traps:
- Feeling undue responsibility for others, a compulsion always to "fix" what ails these people. This is significant, for ministers are typically

seen by nearly all of society as "fixers." But only God can truly "fix" people, as they cooperate with Him.

- Saying "yes" when they mean "no"; being "people-pleasers."
- Doing for others what others are capable of doing for themselves.
- Seeking to be "all things to all people." Many people in vocational Christian service misapply 1 Corinthians 9:22 in a noble effort to "minister" to everyone they can. But they sometimes forget that the context of the verse has to do with evangelism, not with attempting to "fix" every person who has a need. Paul was speaking about adapting his evangelistic approach to Jews and Gentiles, not of compulsively meeting every human being's needs. That is impossible for human beings; only God can meet every person's needs.
- Feeling good about themselves only when they are giving to others.
- Being primarily motivated by interpersonal and social rewards. Rather, we need to be motivated by God's approval (2 Timothy 2:15).
- Feeling exclusively attracted to needy people.
- Feeling bored, empty, and even worthless if there isn't a problem to solve or someone needing help.
- Continually abandoning a schedule or important project for the sake of someone else's needs; "dropping everything" because someone needs "fixing."
- Over-committing themselves and then feeling harassed and under pressure.
- Consistently rejecting praise and yet becoming depressed when none is given.
- Often feeling guilty when spending money on personal needs.
- Fearing rejection (or feeling guilty) if not constantly ministering to others.
- Too easily taking things personally.
- Being overly afraid of making mistakes.
- Being driven by perfectionist, self-imposed standards.

WHAT IS AT THE ROOT OF THESE PROBLEMS?

Each case is unique, but research has exposed these common denominators:

1. *Hidden or repressed anger, often involving unresolved conflicts from the past.* These individuals habitually explode in anger as a way of letting off steam.

2. *Endless living in the fast lane.* The pattern of ceaseless activity, constantly being on the go, and cultivating experiences of great exhilaration and great exhaustion can cause Christian leaders to thrive on risk-taking and even to consider this on-the-edge lifestyle as normative. Then, when temptations come, their spiritual resources have already been drained and they are more likely to fall into sin.

3. *The superstar syndrome.* These individuals thrive on the praise of others and become heroes to their admirers. "Ministry for God" (and the resultant praise) often becomes an escape from family responsibilities and an artificial way to have personal needs met.

4. *Habitually hiding one's own deep needs.* These Christian leaders end up neglecting their own need for intimacy by not allowing themselves to appear human to others. They continue to give to others even when their own emotional "tanks" are empty.

5. *Operating without a personal support system.* No matter where Christian leaders live, in the United States or abroad, they often experience intense stress and loneliness. Not daring to share on a deep level with anyone, they open themselves up to fierce attacks from the Adversary.

6. *Establishing only superficial relationships with others.* In not being real with others and in throwing up barriers to intimacy, these leaders increasingly cut themselves off from support and begin a lonely, downward spiral.

7. Allowing expectations of self and of others to drive one to the point of exhaustion and burnout. These leaders can no longer cope with life's heavy demands. Their lives and ministries no longer have meaning, and they experience hopelessness.

WHAT ARE SOME SOLUTIONS?
First, a Word to Lay Christians
Unwittingly, Christian laypeople may be feeding into the problem. When those in Christian ministry are placed on a pedestal (as discussed in chapter 10), unrealistic expectations are imposed on them. True, those in ministry should be examples, but that does not mean that they must be paragons of perfection. They and their families should be free to be themselves and to enjoy life within biblical parameters without harsh judgment from their followers.

Christian leaders provide encouragement and support for the laity, but they have needs, too. They need the following things from those around them:

- Faithful prayer support
- Respectful treatment
- Encouragement and communication between themselves and their people
- Lightening of the load when possible
- Appreciation expressed verbally and in writing
- Consideration of their reputation even when they aren't present
- Respect for their privacy
- Freedom from unnecessary demands on their time and energy
- Protection from the "appearance of evil" with the opposite sex

We are too often unaware that our spiritual leaders struggle and sometimes fall. God's plan is to build, and rebuild, them. The road may be arduous, but the Lord promises, "I know the plans I have for you . . . plans to prosper you and not to harm you, plans to give you hope and a future" (Jeremiah 29:11 NIV). Another promise says, "'I will satisfy the priests with abundance, and my people will be filled with my bounty,' declares the Lord" (Jeremiah 31:14 NIV).

Help for the Christian Worker

1. *You are not alone.* All the heroes in God's hall of fame struggled. Some fell. We don't have to fall. God Himself says, "The temptations in your life are no different from what others experience" (1 Corinthians 10:13 NLT).

2. *There is hope.* The saying goes, "The darkest hour is the hour before the dawn." You may have struggled for a long time and failed again and again, but a fresh start, a new hope, is always available. God hasn't given up on you, so don't give up on yourself!

But as for me, I watch in hope for the Lord,
I wait for God my Savior;
my God will hear me. . . .
Though I have fallen, I will rise. Though I sit in darkness,
the Lord will be my light. (Micah 7:7–8 NIV)

3. *You cannot change on your own.* You may be able to make a change for a few days or a few weeks, but you need outside help for long-lasting change. Primarily, of course, it's the Holy Spirit's power you need, but God never intended for you to struggle alone on the human level. It's okay to need someone else. Although ultimate responsibility rests on you, a relationship of accountability and support with a godly brother or sister (of the same sex) can help assure you the victory. Being tempted is not sinful; the sinfulness lies in how that temptation is handled. "Share each other's burdens, and in this way obey the law of Christ" (Galatians 6:2 NLT).

4. *Seek a new depth in your relationship with God.* Commit to living a holy life free from those attractions that on the surface may seem to be harmless but are actually debilitating. Involvement in sin will corrode your inner being and render you ineffective in your life and ministry. "Therefore, I urge you, brothers, in view of God's mercy, to offer your bodies as living

sacrifices, holy and pleasing to God—this is your spiritual act of worship" (Romans 12:1 NIV).

5. *Seek a new depth of emotional intimacy in your marriage.* Cultivate the habit of openly exchanging your thoughts and feelings at a deep level. Let yourself be vulnerable with your spouse. Work toward allowing yourself to say such things as: "Sometimes I'm lonely." "Sometimes I get discouraged." "Sometimes I feel shut out of your life." "I don't always do it right. Can you help me?"

As you mutually encourage and nurture each other, neither of you will be as likely to look outside your marriage for satisfaction of your inner needs. As you grow in intimacy with each other, you will grow closer to the Lord.

6. *Make a checklist of sinful practices or seemingly neutral practices that do not contribute to a godly life.* Be sure to include thoughts, fantasies, feelings, and actions that stimulate or gratify you sexually. Also, include TV programs or magazines that may not seem overtly pornographic but still appeal to the flesh. These programs and magazines may not appear to be all that bad, but you can become enslaved to them if you are not careful.

7. *Don't give up.* Satan will try to convince you that it's a hopeless cause. Daily encourage yourself, and receive encouragement from the Lord and others. "God is faithful. He will not allow the temptation to be more than you can stand. When you are tempted, he will show you a way out so that you can endure" (1 Corinthians 10:13 NLT).

8. *Write down your commitment, and keep it in a visible place where you'll see it often.* Commit on a moment-by-moment basis. That is the way effective change comes about. "Your word is a lamp to my feet and a light for my path" (Psalm 119:105 NIV).

9. *Continually be renewed in your mind by meditating on Scripture.* Memorize it. Flood your mind with God's Word, for it is your greatest weapon

against the onslaughts of the evil one. It will enable you to put to death the first thoughts of temptation. "Do not conform any longer to the pattern of this world, but be transformed by the renewing of your mind" (Romans 12:2 NIV).

10. *Take time for recreation, enjoyment, fun, and, most important, exercise.* A balanced life that includes diversion will bring untold spiritual, emotional, and physical benefits. After a time of ministry, the apostles reported to Jesus their impressive accomplishments. In fact, they were so busy they didn't even have time to eat. Jesus saw their predicament, and in loving concern He advised, "Come with me by yourselves to a quiet place and get some rest" (Mark 6:31 NIV).

Appendix B

RESOURCE LIST FROM THE AUTHORS

Carder, Dave

Torn Asunder Workbook: Recovering from an Extramarital Affair. Chicago: Moody Publishers, 2008.

Close Calls: What Adulterers Want You to Know about Protecting Your Marriage. Chicago: Moody Publishers, 2008.

Carder, Dave, and Duncan Jaenicke

Torn Asunder: Recovering from an Extramarital Affair. Chicago: Moody Publishers, 2008.

Cloud, Henry

How to Get a Date Worth Keeping. Grand Rapids: Zondervan, 2005.

Integrity: The Courage to Meet the Demands of Reality. New York: HarperCollins, 2006.

9 Things You Simply Must Do to Succeed in Love and Life. Nashville: Thomas Nelson, 2004.

The One Life Solution: Reclaim Your Personal Life While Achieving Greater Professional Success. New York: HarperCollins, 2008.

The Secret Things of God: Unlocking the Treasures Reserved For You. New York: Howard, 2007.

Cloud, Henry, and John Townsend
Boundaries: When to Say Yes, When to Say No to Take Control of Your Life. Grand Rapids: Zondervan, 1992.

God Will Make a Way: What to Do When You Don't Know What to Do. Brentwood, Tennessee: Integrity, 2003.

How People Grow: What the Bible Reveals about Personal Growth. Grand Rapids: Zondervan, 2004.

How to Have That Difficult Conversation You've Been Avoiding. Grand Rapids: Zondervan, 2005.

It's Not My Fault: The No-Excuses Plan for Overcoming the Effects of People, Circumstances or DNA and Enjoying God's Best. Nashville: Thomas Nelson, 2007.

The Mom Factor. Grand Rapids: Zondervan, 1998.

Safe People: How to Find Relationships That Are Good for You and Avoid Those That Aren't. Grand Rapids: Zondervan, 1996.

Henslin, Earl
This Is Your Brain in Love. Nashville: Thomas Nelson, 2010.

This Is Your Brain on Joy. Nashville: Thomas Nelson, 2009.

Townsend, John
Hiding from Love. Grand Rapids: Zondervan, 1996.

Leadership Beyond Reason: How Great Leaders Succeed by Harnessing the Power of their Values, Feelings, and Intuition. Nashville: Thomas Nelson, 2009.

Loving People: How to Love and Be Loved. Nashville: Thomas Nelson, 2008.

Where is God?: Finding His Presence, Purpose, and Power in Difficult Times. Nashville: Thomas Nelson, 2009.

Who's Pushing Your Buttons: Handling the Difficult People in Your Life. Nashville: Thomas Nelson, 2007.

Appendix C

The Twelve Steps of Alcoholics Anonymous*

1. We admitted we were powerless over our dependencies—that our lives had become unmanageable.

2. Came to believe that a Power greater than ourselves could restore us to sanity.

3. Made a decision to turn our will and our lives over to the care of God as we understood Him.

4. Made a searching and fearless moral inventory of ourselves.

5. Admitted to God, to ourselves, and to another human being the exact nature of our wrongs.

6. Were entirely ready to have God remove all these defects of character.

7. Humbly asked Him to remove our shortcomings.

8. Made a list of all persons we had harmed, and became willing to make amends to them all.

9. Made direct amends to such people wherever possible, except when to do so would injure them or others.

10. Continued to take personal inventory and when we were wrong promptly admitted it.

11. Sought through prayer and meditation to improve our conscious contact with God as we understood Him, praying only for knowledge of His will for us and the power to carry that out.

12. Having had a spiritual awakening as the result of these steps, we tried to carry this message to alcoholics, and to practice these principles in all our affairs.

*The Twelve Steps are reprinted with permission of Alcoholics Anonymous World Services, Incorporated. Permission to reprint and adapt the Twelve Steps does not mean that A.A. has reviewed or approved the contents of any publication that reprints the Twelve Steps, nor that A.A. agrees with the views expressed therein. A.A. is a program of recovery from alcoholism. Use of the Twelve Steps in connection with programs that are patterned after A.A. but which address other problems does not imply otherwise.

About the Authors

Dave Carder currently serves as pastor for counseling ministries at the First Evangelical Free Church of Fullerton, California. He holds graduate degrees in Biblical Literature and in Counseling Psychology as well as the Michigan Limited License in Psychology and the Marriage and Family Therapy license in California. Dave has published five books, one of which won The Gold Medallion Award in Personal Evangelism in 1993. Dave and his wife, Ronnie, have four adult children and five grandchildren. In their spare time they enjoy jogging.

Facebook: Dave Carder—author and speaker
www.TornAsunder.org
www.DaveCarder.com

Dr. Henry Cloud is a clinical psychologist, leadership consultant, bestselling author, and communicator. He has written or coauthored more than twenty books, including the bestselling *Boundaries*, *Integrity*, *9 Things You Simply Must Do To Succeed in Love and Life*, and *Necessary Endings*. Dr. Cloud is the cohost of the nationally syndicated radio program *New Life Live*. He lives in Los Angeles with his wife, Tori, and their two daughters.

www.drcloud.com
Twitter.com/drhenrycloud
Facebook.com/drhenrycloud

Dr. Earl Henslin is a clinical psychologist and licensed marriage and family therapist, and former faculty at the Rosemead Graduate School of Psychology at Biola University. He is the author or coauthor of ten books and numerous professional articles. He helped found Overcomers Outreach to help churches establish support groups. Dr. Henslin leads seminars and retreats, coaches executives, and helps businesses become "brain-healthy organizations." In association with research pioneer Daniel G. Amen, M.D., Dr. Henslin has spent fourteen years integrating brain imaging into the treatment of psychological, physical, and spiritual problems in his counseling practice in Brea, California. Dr. Henslin has four adult children and two granddaughters.

www.drhenslin.com
Twitter: drhenslin
Facebook.com/group.php?gid=46688717236

Dr. John Townsend is a psychologist, relational expert, business consultant, and leadership coach. He has written or cowritten more than twenty books, selling five million copies, including the bestselling *Boundaries, Leadership Beyond Reason*, and *Handling Difficult People*. Dr. Townsend is a co-host of the nationally syndicated talk show *New Life Live*. John is a visiting professor at Dallas Theological Seminary and is clinical director of the American Association of Christian Counselors. He is active on the board of directors of Mustard Seed Ranch, a residential program for abused children. John, his wife, and their children reside in Newport Beach, California. John's passion is playing in a band that performs at southern California lounges and venues.

www.drtownsend.com
Facebook.com/DoctorJohnTownsend
Twitter.com/drjohntownsend

TORN ASUNDER

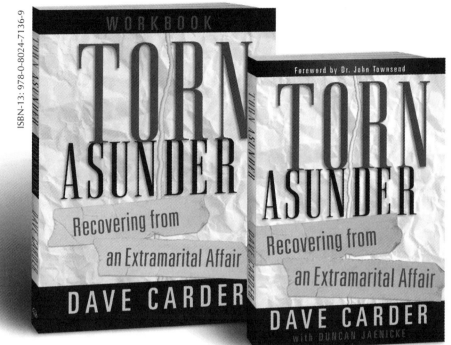

ISBN-13: 978-0-8024-7136-9

ISBN-13: 978-0-8024-7135-2

Infidelity is at crisis levels even within the church. No marriage is immune despite apparent moral convictions. Dave Carder wrote *Torn Asunder* to offer couples hope, healing, and encouragement in the face of adultery. He divides his book into first helping readers understand extramarital affairs and then offering healing for marriages dealing with this betrayal. This refreshed and updated edition is an excellent resource for pastors, leaders, and lay people.

The workbook allows couples to work through and apply the material presented in *Torn Asunder*. It is organized into daily twenty-minute exercises initiated by each spouse on alternating days. Because this tragic situation is not easily resolved, it is imperative to get couples on the road to healing and oneness.

MOODY
PUBLISHERS

moodypublishers.com

CLOSE CALLS

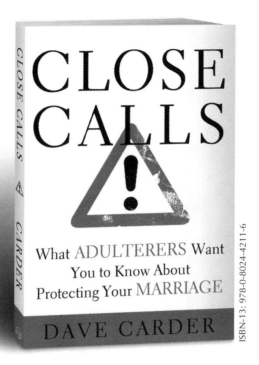

Never say never; because just when you think your marriage is safe from adultery is when you may be the most vulnerable. Dave Carder, counselor, author of the bestselling *Torn Asunder* (100,000 in print), and a sought-after expert on issues of infidelity, has spent more than 30 years counseling spouses trapped in adultery. Now, with eye-opening stories, clinical insights, and up-to-date data, he reveals what adulterers learned the hard way–and want the rest of us to know. For example, every spouse has a "Dangerous Partner Profile" of the kind of person who tempts them. *Close Calls* should be on every church leader's and marriage counselor's required reading list. Includes charts and assessments.

MOODY
PUBLISHERS

moodypublishers.com

WHEN LIFE IS HARD

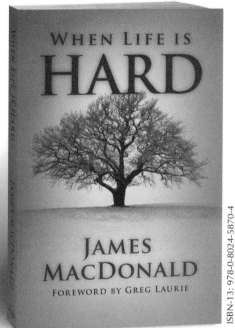

ISBN-13: 978-0-8024-5870-4

When life is hard, you know, really hard, we often spend all our time pleading, begging, yelling, refusing, and questioning. While none of these things are necessarily unusual, they are missing the ultimate point. When life is hard, when things get ugly, when all hope seems to be lost, that is when we are able to display the superiority of the life lived in God. It is in those moments of despair, when we question what is happening, when we don't know what to do, when some trials never seem to end, that we can lean most heavily into God's promises and truths.

Trusted pastor James MacDonald helps us to understand what we should do now. Should we just try to weather the storm? Or is there something greater in God's vision for these difficulties?

MOODY
PUBLISHERS

AN ANCHOR FOR THE SOUL

ISBN-13: 978-0-8024-1536-3

People have honest doubts and questions about God that deserve solid answers. How do we explain the gospel of Jesus Christ in a way we can all understand? Ray Pritchard has updated this bestselling presentation of the gospel in a clear, straightforward way using simple language and clear Scripture references.

An Anchor for the Soul is written with doubters, seekers, and skeptics in mind. It answers questions such as: What is God like? How can I know Him? Who is Jesus and what did He do? What does it mean to be a Christian? Through stories and illustrations, Pastor Pritchard very personally, yet gently, challenges his readers with the Good News of Jesus Christ.

MOODY
PUBLISHERS